If You Ever Feel Like Coming Home

Nicholas Talerico

A big thank you to all of my readers.

This is for you.

Contents

If You Ever Feel Like Coming Home

I Can't Wait to See 18

I Don't Care 19

I'm Your Redneck Crazy 20

I Must Be a Fool 21

Transcription 22

You Can Check This 23

I Turned On the Radio 24

As Little as Possible 25

I Will Not Give Up 26

I Found a Lunchbox in My... 27

So, You Want to Be A... 28

Gone for Good 29

It's A Good Thing 30

Life Is More Than a Dream 31

All in All 32

I Sit Inside the Shell of the Old Me 33

Come and Get Me 34

I'm Gonna Be 35

Junk Mail 36

Hadda Be 37

You Might Get in Trouble 38

I Don't Wanna Say 39

It's Not Just You 40

Another Chapter Closed 41
Clearly Not Interested.. 42
I am Just a Guy... 43
You Stumble 44
Reading into Things & Reality.. 45
Consequences 46
It's So Good 47
What Could've Been 48
I Think About It All The Time.. 49
Oh, It's So Tight 50
A Girl From the Post Office 51
The Things You Say 52
I Might Be a Fool to Bet It All.. 53
Just So You Know 54
Going Out and Coming Back... 55
Looking for You.. 56
Laying My Hand On the Radio 57
The Roommate From Hell... 58
Paying the Price 59
From Past Events 60
A Note Full of Love 61
No One Cares.. 63
The Heart of a Poet... 64
Make Me an Offer 65
I've Opened My Eyes to Something New............................ 66
Wish You Were Here... 67
My Facebook Friends.. 68
Unfulfilled Desire 69
I Keep a Piece of You in Me 70
I Need Your Smile 71
It Was Like They Opened Up (A Portal to the Past)........... 72
Cut Me Some Slack 73

Little Dirty Girl...74
Yesterday's Footprints 75
I'll Be There 76
A Book on the Shelf 77
God is in My…...79
Letters in the Library 80
If I Had to Choose Only One...81
Dirty Sex..82
If I Had Not Let You Go 83
Wet & Charming 84
I Know, I Know...85
Get ... Out of My Life!!...86
(God Must Have Spent) A Little More Time On You 87
I'm Living on Borrowed Time 88
Stop The Hoax..89
I'll Kick Your Butt (If You Pinch Me) 90
Every Day Is Precious 91
I Need You Here 92
A Man Loses Only What He Has 93
I'm Not Bipolar (I'm Multipolar) 94
Wise Motherhood 95
Every Great Discovery, I Ever Made….............................96
You Are Nowhere 97
Cards I Was Dealt..98
Signature..99

My Contribution

What Might Have Been 102
I See Pride, I See Power 103
Boom, Boom, Boom, (It Could've Been You) 104
When Tomorrow Comes..105
Can't Go Home 106

I Thought I Told You...107

Temporarily Unavailable (lyrics to My Song).................108

It's Not Like, I'm Poor 109

Still Do I Keep My…? 110

The Right Side of History 111

Before Winter, I'll Have a New 112

I Write What I Think 113

I Don't Know How She Does It, But… 114

Wall Street Goes Global...115

I Am Not Your Victim 116

It'll Be a Thousand Years Before I… 117

Tie Me Up, Make Me Scream 118

I Need a New Prescription 119

I'll Give You My Love, If You Give Me… 120

Politically Correct Yes, But I… 121

Ready or Not..122

You Can Bribe Me With 123

I Am an American, I'm Not a Terrorist........................124

In The End, I Became..125

Growing Up Poorly 126

Kinky Boots..128

My Shame, Couldn't Let Me.....................................129

The Reviewers Are Saying 130

Dear Me, I Hate You...131

With His Pistol in His Hand 132

The First Five Pages..133

I'm Thirsty for Your..135

I Didn't Write This...136

Don't Hit Up My Line 137

Today Ain't the Day..138

She Always Knew 139

Damn You Lil Hoochie Momma.................................140

The Private Nightmare with an Ending..........................141

If You Were My Girl...142

I'll Stop Being a…...143

Love Shouldn't Be a Slap in the Face...........................144

Out of the Blue..145

Looking Out, Looking In 146

I'm On a One-Way Ticket To..147

Stop Wasting Your Time On 148

You Are Too Young To..149

Girls Are Quick and Dirty When it Comes to… 150

It's Not Very Often..151

Modern Love..152

Hey Country Girl, This Country Boy 153

Under Construction..154

It Was Just..155

Independently I Speak..156

Today I Realized 157

I Run and I Run 158

Miss Popularity..159

You Must Be Crazy..160

But, I Want to Know 161

Is She Available? 162

The Right Side of Hello, The Wrong Side of Goodbye .163

Typewriter Rodeo...164

This Book Has Been Through a Lot.................................165

Hell Is the Moment 166

The Library of Souls...167

Blue Dreams..168

The Deepest Well...169

Walk to Fight for Suicide...170

Hunger to Save the Epilepsy 171

The New Boyfriend from My Cheating Girlfriend.......172

Every Single Thing from My Homie and I.....................173
The Sexy Lingerie 174
Oh, No!!!! Not Another Poem 175
Every Man in His Day 176
When I Am in Trouble 177
It's Not as Easy as You 178
All She Wants Is That...179
Breathing In and Breathing Out......................................180
Everything But The 181
A Black Boo...182
Butterfly Kisses 183
I'm Just a Kid From The Projects......................................184

The Book of the Month

The Book of the Month 186
Hot Content 187
She's My Baby Girl..188
I Make My Husband 189
Welcome to My Life 190
I Love Being Honest...191
Good Looking Out, Good Looking In 192
Oh, The Places You'll Go!...193
Temporarily Blocked..194
Somebody Scream...195
Living With The Devil 196
If I Get Locked Up..197
Digital Storytelling...198
From Street Life to Country Life......................................199
Wherever You Are (My Love Will Find You) 200
I Feel Like a Retired Rockstar...201
Full, Full, Full of Love 202
You're Tired, You're Poor..203

Fuck Me 204

Yours 205

Awful Poetry From What I Have Read............................ 206

Orchestrating Love... 207

On This Battlefield Called Life 208

She's Just Too Hot 209

My Booty Is 210

When It's Over You'll Be.. 211

My Current Occupation 212

Here Fishy, Fishy, Fish 213

Yep—Fake, Fake, Fake 214

An Honest Homeless Person 215

Your Orgasm Inside Me.. 216

I Married You, Not Your Family................................... 217

This Southern Boy Is Thinking About............................ 218

Country Girl Lawd Have Mercy................................... 219

From Society Page to the Front Page............................ 220

I'd Like to Fill Her Up (But My Thing's Too Small) 221

It's Like Livin' in A.. 222

Redneck Country Girl 223

It Is to Be... 224

Do Not Be Ashamed 225

She's 226

I Wanna Be Your Cowboy.. 227

The Storyteller... 228

The Young Prostitute.. 229

The Dream Catcher.. 230

Love Is Like Whiskey 231

Baby 'O' Baby 232

Everybody Loves My Baby 233

Putting In The Seed... 234

Sidewalk Celebrity.. 235

The Thought of Someone Else 236
To Be Liked by You, Would Be 237
Baby (Gimmie A Little Lovin') 238
I Reckon It'll Be 239
I Was Thirsty, She Was Hot 240
My Heart Is Not... 241
Haven't Slept With A Woman.. 242
(Do Not) Sell Me Out Baby... 243
This I Write, Mix Ink with Tears 244
The Unfaithful Wife 245
The Greyhound Affair.. 246
Just A Kid from Kankakee 247
As I Ride, As I Ride (Down That Road Called Life) 248
Written While Drunk 249
Riddle from the Book 250
When I Got You, I Thought 252
My Life Ain't Nothin' (From a Nightmare of a Dream)253
Little Black Boys in a Southern Jail.............................. 254
Home Is Where the Heart Is 255
I Want You to Have His Baby.. 256
Sex Is on Your Mind.. 257
She's My 5150 258
Stay Away from My Chick.. 259
Makin' You Mine 260
Don't Eat With Your Dirty Hands................................ 261
I Got Carried Away in the Moment.............................. 262
Southern on Display 263
Supercalifragilisticexpialidocious 264
The Dirty Thought.. 265
When I Grow Up, I'm Going to Be Like........................ 266

(God Must Have Spent)
A Little More Time On You

The Original Nudist 268
She'll Make Your 269
While Tracking Mud Into The House...........................270
But, Tomorrow I Will Redeem My...............................271
The Book Performers 272
I'm Spontaneously in Love 273
If Only She Could..274
I'm Just an Asshole 275
I Have This Letter You Wrote Me...............................276
She's That Kind of Gal Who Kept..............................277
Must Have Been Yesterday......................................278
I'll Find A Chance To..279
I Still Appreciate You 280
I Used to Tell You 281
I No Longer See You As...282
Your Answer Is...283
I'm Standing On 284
Backwoods Booty..285
You Know What Time It Is When… 286
Pretty, Pretty, Little Liar....................................287
Don't Just Listen 288
People Say I'm Black 289
Seriously, Between Us..290
My Flag, My Roots, My Camo In My Boots 291
Excuse Me, Pardon Me Miss......................................292
One Tree Hill 293
I'll Just Keep Writing...294
My Craigslist Dream..295
Broken Crayons 296

Bam! It's A Good Thing! (That! I Did It)........................297

Hip-Hop Isn't Dead...298

I Still Believe in Christmas.......................................299

Cotton Candy Christmas 300

Rumor Has It...301

She'll Always Be...302

It's Not Like Her..303

Changing Me...304

Motivation Speech..305

Love is Love..306

It Was Only A Kiss 307

Low Self-Esteem 308

Black Girls Rock 309

Holy Thursday 310

So and So Is Lying 311

It's Always the Wife...312

Be Like Me..313

You're Not Talking..314

Love Unknown 315

I Found A Girl to Be in Love 316

Jenny Kissed Me 317

Bonnie & Clyde 318

Verse Idea 319

She Tosses That (Boom, Boom)..................................320

Liar, Liar, Pants On Fire...321

Reflections From An Abused Kid 322

My Life # 5..323

No Such Thing As A Bad Kid 324

My Life # 6..325

Gossip Friendship Talk..326

Her Face, Her Tongue, Her Ass 327

The Girl He Likes..328

I Didn't Want It To Be A Craigslist Moment 329
You've Got To Be 330
I'm Not Bigfoot Where You Can… 331
Uncle Sam Wants You To…. 332
A Clownlike Fool.................333
O My Great Idiot 334
Between This Wish and That Wish 335
From Time to Time.................336
I Had This Wet Dream.................337
While You Were Out.................338
Dirt On My Boots 339
If You Ask Me.................340
I'm Ok, You're My Parents.................341
Just When I Thought… 342
I Was Too Young To Notice 343
Under My Bed 344
Sometimes In The Summer There's.................345
When She Walks Right By Me.................346
This Time, I Thought 347

If You Ever Feel Like Coming Home

Written By,

Nicholas Talerico

I Can't Wait to See

I can't wait to see the new me
I can't wait to see you when I reach heaven
I can't wait to see my own wings
I can't wait to see you again
I can't wait to see Jesus for the first time
I can't wait to see the golden gates
I can't wait to see; I can't wait to see.

I Don't Care

I don't care
It's all for me
It's all for me
I don't even know what it is
What is wrong with you?
And what's in your hands?
I'm on the same page as
you, you dumbass
No man, fuck you man
I don't care, I don't care.

I'm Your Redneck Crazy

I'm your redneck crazy that will say read my lips
I'm your redneck crazy that would say kiss my redneck ass
I'm your redneck crazy country boy through and through
I'm your redneck crazy who can be your ride or die boo
I'm your redneck crazy that doesn't mind getting muddy
I'm your redneck crazy that will stand for the red, white, and
    blue
I'm your redneck crazy that is your officially true blue
I'm your redneck crazy who sings the blues
I'm your redneck crazy who keeps his Bible next to you
I'm your redneck crazy, I'm your redneck crazy.

I Must Be a Fool

I must be a fool to fall for you again
I must be a fool to think that you right
I must be a fool to lose it all over nothing
I must be a fool to write this new poem
I must be a fool to ask for a lifeline
I must be a fool, a fool for you.

Transcription

I forbid you not to touch me
I believed you, you rejected me
I denied all allegations against me
I know more than I should be
My transcription is my vocabulary
This is my, this is my transcription.

You Can Check This

You can check this
You can check that
You can check all of
it if you want to,
and stick it up your ass.

I Turned On the Radio

I turned on the radio
to hear what's up,
but all I heard
was nothing but gun shot
sounds, people crying,
another person dying;
this world is so depressing.
I turned on the radio
just to hear a song that
I wanted to enjoy.

As Little as Possible

As little as possible
As much as needed
Too much information
can lead to the wrong person,
so sit down, be quiet,
and give as much information
as needed.

I Will Not Give Up

I will not give up on God's hope and beliefs
I will not give up on anyone who needs help
I will not give up on you when you need it the most
I will not give up on chasing my dreams
I will not give up when other's will try to get me to
I will not give up no matter how hard I fall.

I Found a Lunchbox in My...

I found a lunchbox in my locker-room
I found a lunchbox in my closet
I found a lunchbox in my safety box
I found a lunchbox in my desk
I found a lunchbox in my refrigerator
I found a lunchbox in my bookstore
I found a lunchbox, I found a lunchbox.

So, You Want to Be A…

So, you want to be a writer, then write something great.
So, you want to be a singer, than sing something with
    passion.
So, you want to be an actor, then act like you never have
    before.
So, you want to be a world star, than steal someone else's
    shine.
So, you want to be a person with love, then give lots of it.
So, you want to be anything you want, then go out and do it.

Gone for Good

Gone for good with mixed
messages and offhand remarks
miraculously still secreting hope
while the language filled with dope,
the dictionary stolen from the local
junior high school bootlegged billions
to give false hope, but now that
he's gone for good, I can take back
what he has finally took.

It's A Good Thing

It's a good thing that
some of y'all's ego
blew up like Snapchat;
maybe next time you should
try to chit-chat, oh look
a postcard from the future
that says stop that,
quit trying to be a copycat,
that might be the last time
you will come at me
and it's a really good thing
that you will never be like me.

Life Is More Than a Dream

Life is more than just a dream
Reflections of a time I couldn't speak
As words left the proof I was so weak
Life surrounds us all with just a blink
But I couldn't lie if this is the
true legacy of just me and in the end
life is more than just a fairytale dream.

All in All

My letters are opened
my e-mails deleted
but I'm not defeated
nor even heated
for they'll never stop me
from communicating my habits
another spoken word
can be added
all in all, who knows
I just might be savaged
So, watch out for Lenny Kravitz.

I Sit Inside the Shell of the Old Me

I'm disgusted
it's unbelievable
I sit inside the shell
of the old me
the mind is like a butterfly
it's everybody's dream
inside out, backwards, and forwards
it's still my dream
yes, I'm disgusted, yes, It's unbelievable
but yet, I sit inside the shell
of the old me.

Come and Get Me

I can make it bounce by myself
fuck the honor roll I'm on the
head of the dean's list it doesn't
matter if I'm country I'm going to be
running like Obama when he left
the White House come and get me
I don't give a shit I'll bust his ass like
he did to me so if you're going to
come then come and get me you fool.

I'm Gonna Be

I'm gonna be a dad
I'm gonna be an old man
I'm gonna be the best I can be
I'm gonna be the next best thing
I'm gonna be an author
I'm gonna be a musician
I'm gonna be your Valentine
I'm gonna be your ride or die
I'm gonna be, I'm gonna be.

Junk Mail

I received in mail
invites, subscriber's,
monthly reviews,
foundation misdelivered;
you might get in trouble
just to spam others'
junk mail, junk mail
old and boring news
hit that delete button and
throw it in the trash
junk mail, junk mail, I just
received it in my junk mail.

Hadda Be

Chorus x2
hadda be playing
on the jukebox
hadda be written in
the library books
footnoted on the windshield
there's a storm coming through
hadda be coming back home to you
yeah, hadda be heading home real soon.

You Might Get in Trouble

You might get in trouble if you do some stupid shit
You might get in trouble if you ask too many questions
You might get in trouble if you try to challenge an authority
You might get in trouble if you back-talk to the elderly
You might get in trouble if you break the rules
You might get in trouble if you copyright someone's usage
You might get in trouble; you might get in trouble.

I Don't Wanna Say

I don't wanna say I'm sorry cause I know I might be wrong
I don't wanna say I love you unless I really mean it
I don't wanna say I was wrong but I knew it was true
I don't wanna say I told you so then it turns out to be a lie
I don't wanna say that I have made regrets even though I
    never take it back
I don't wanna say that I care when really I do care
I don't wanna say that it's over when I know it's not the case
I don't wanna say, I really don't wanna say.

It's Not Just You

It's not just you who I feel sorry for
It's not just you who didn't tell the truth
It's not just you who made poor decisions
It's not just you who swore from the holy Bible
It's not just you who made a promise
It's not just you who said I hate you
It's not just you who wanted more from life
It's not just you who gave everything that they had
It's not just you who walked right out on you
It's not just you, it's not just you.

Another Chapter Closed

Another chapter closed
Another gate opened
Another chapter page was turned to claim
another story that took his glory
Another glorious day we praised in his name,
but in the end it's just another day.

Clearly Not Interested

I'm clearly not interested in being your woman
I'm clearly not interested in being unfaithful
I'm clearly not interested in wanting to have a kid with you
I'm clearly not interested in anything that has to do with
    your drama
I'm clearly not interested in being your ride or die
I'm clearly not interested in how you think I am yours to
    keep
I'm clearly not interested in being flirtatious with you
I'm clearly not interested in wanting anything you want in
    life
I'm clearly not interested in wanting to go out on a date with
    you
I'm clearly not interested; I'm clearly not interested.

I am Just a Guy

I am just a guy, I can't walk on water, and
I'm no man's savior; so, I can't save you, I'm sorry.
Inside and out I am still the same guy
who loved you as much as he tried. Yes, I believe
in kindness, mercy, compassion, forgiveness,
sisterhood, brotherhood, family, country, love,
hope, faith, and God, but I know the grass is not
greener on the other side; then again, I am just a guy.

You Stumble

You stumble, you fall flat as you snapped
your photo you were in a hurry, left without
warning, now my picture is somewhere in
this world with the internet popping up
everywhere. I can now search for it anywhere
as you stumble, you fall; I'm glad you took
that photo cause in the end, I will see soon in all.

Reading into Things & Reality

Reading into things & reality
It's the end of the line sadly
I felt sorry for you, when I knew
all along that you had to pay your dues,
but in the end I guess this is for
the best for me and you, as you know
yes, I am still in love with you.

Consequences

There is always a price to pay
when only a fool believes that
they are right and wrong but truth
is pretty soon, it's the end of the line
doing everything wrong from left to right
will have them wishing that they
were wrong but in the end it's there;
consequences that got them there from
the beginning of the start.

It's So Good

it's so good you continually bless me
it's so good to feel his presence with me
it's so good to know that I praise his glory
it's so good to feel not empty
it's so good to know how much he loves me
it's so good to know he's holy
it's so good, it's so good to me.

What Could've Been

What could've been should have been
What could've been never has been
What could've been has been forgotten
What could've been has been taken for granted
What could've been never was
What could've been; what could've been.

I Think About It All The Time

I think about it all the time and yet I don't listen
I think about it all the time and it still scares me
I think about it all the time and it never really clicks on me
I think about it all the time and I can't seem to shake it off
I think about it all the time and I am still puzzled
I think about it all the time and yet it hasn't sunk through me
I think about it all the time and yet that's why we have
    consequences.

Oh, It's So Tight

Oh, it's so tight
that's what she said
going full throttle
once every single night
Oh, it's so tight
well baby at least I know your
riding and griping it right
Oh, it's so tight, oh it's so tight
yeah this is gonna be
one hell of a night
Oh, it's so tight, this is gonna
be the last for the night.

A Girl From the Post Office

A girl from the post office
that I fell in love with that
girl right there yeah the girl,
is not mine I'll be checking
the post offices working time
hoping she'll be mine thank
God she is so damn fine country
girl for life I wanna make her
my wife that's right a girl from
the post office oh my, my, my.

The Things You Say

The things you say, the things you write
The things you say, the things you whisper
The things you say, the things you make me smile
The things you say, the things you do to make me wonder
The things you say, the things that make this man's dreams
    come true
The things you say, the things when you don't try to change me
The things you say, the things that will forever be with me
The things you say, the things that make me stay.

I Might Be a Fool to Bet It All

I might be a fool to bet it all
for something more than this
I hope you know that as long
as I'm alive, I'll always seek
to win your kiss and in the end
I can guarantee that you will
have my final respect for me.

Just So You Know

Just so you know I am playing for keeps
Just so you know I am not yours to throw away
Just so you know I still love you
Just so you know I broke the rules
Just so you know I am forever single
Just so you know I will never stop believing
Just so you know, just so you know.

Going Out and Coming Back

Going out and coming back
open all night just so you
know that's not even right
I said it once and I'll say it
Again, and a thousand more times,
going out and coming back
this time it will be the last
going out and coming back
farewell to you my guest.

Looking for You

I've been looking for you
looking for you, tick-tock
tick-tock just like a clock
I've been looking all over for you
I've been looking just for you.

Laying My Hand On the Radio

Laying my hand on the radio
while listening to the stereo
driving around on a dirt road
hey country girl, this country boy
turn up that song by Mario
hey, hey don't be shy now
this is your favorite song girl
so lay your hand on my radio
and rock out with this southern
boy charm, girl.

The Roommate From Hell

I like the place, and I like you
if you like me, I could just do this now
said from the roommate from hell
I have everything I need
said from the roommate from hell
A few months went by and it went from
good to straight to hell I said
then my roommate said to me well, you don't
have this house anymore, this house is
my house said from the worst roommate ever
as if he said to me and my lady buddy,
I'm living here too, she's asked you to go,
I'm asking you to go, I'll ask you one more time,
or I'll remove you myself like a master
in history who's got a story to tell
as I instated that this is the worst roommate from hell.

Paying the Price

I am paying the price for entering my life
I am paying the price for believing your trust
I am paying the price for everything you haven't done nice
I am paying the price for a broken kind of love
I am paying the price that I wish I can take back
I am paying the price for every mistake that was made
I am paying the price hoping for forgiveness' sake
I am paying the price please give me a second chance.

From Past Events

From past events like a
bank account emptied of love
overdrawn and completely exposed
once filled with dividends and growth
is now on the verge of being closed
from past events to being currently
temporarily unavailable; I hope that
one day she will never be miserable.

A Note Full of Love

A note full of love but
so far away you captured
my attention by true feelings
I expressed without regret
I let you know my true
intentions to make you mine.

A note full of love that
was truly blind when
you smiled it created
the sweetest memory
like moments of conversation
in my southern history.

A note full of love that
instantly made my heart
melt it sounded like a
metallic waterfall beknown
you and me.

And a note full of love that
can make me an offer that
I can't refuse it's much
greater to find out loving you
was always free than to find out
it's worth millions that I can
dig deep for my passion and feelings
about, you are my true blue and a
beautiful note full of love for you.

No One Cares

No one cares about him
No one cares about her
No one cares about us
No one cares if we are even alive
No one cares or tries to understand
No one cares even if we die
No one cares about our feelings
No one cares, no one cares.

The Heart of a Poet

The heart of a poet at times shows their sorrows seem to spill
out onto the page

The heart of a poet seems to spill out onto the page

The heart of a poet, simple call of a Whip-Poor-Will can fill
them with flee

The heart of a poet may find the beauty that others overlook

The heart of a poet has a poet's view of a person that goes
beyond skin deep

The heart of a poet and the beauty of one's heart is not
considered cheap

The heart of a poet and their love is boundless and without
restrictions

The heart of a poet comes from nothing to something

The heart of a poet is a bonfire hero who chases his shadows

The heart of a poet was born an original, who never died as a
copy.

Make Me an Offer

Make me an offer that I can't refuse
Make me an offer that's more precious than gold
Make me an offer that's valuable to others
Make me an offer that can be recollected until covered in
    dust
Make me an offer that is a deal breaker
Make me an offer that's a take it or leave it
Make me an offer, make me an offer.

I've Opened My Eyes to Something New

I've opened my eyes to something new
hope it sees me for what it's through
nothing lasts forever so keep that in mind
know what you're looking for when
the time is right and if you play your cards
just right you'll find out its worth millions
by the end of this night someone didn't
pay attention when his heart isn't right
lions and tigers and bears, oh my! Hope to
include you sometime as I've opened my eyes
to something new.

Wish You Were Here

The summer nights are filled
with an artic chill cold is my bed, home, and heart
without you near missing you is like
searching for the Lovers Stream
my imagination paints a picture in my mind,
that plays tricks on me; wish you were here
I tell this story to you now, because it needs to grow
It's not some great performance, or some
act put up for show; I'll tell you this my love
for there are reasons, I must go little nothing
means everything when I wish you were here to
rescue me wish you were here, I really
wish you were here.

My Facebook Friends

My Facebook friends are fake
My Facebook friends are drama
My Facebook friends are assholes
My Facebook friends are Facebook bitches
My Facebook friends are over the limit
My Facebook friends are never the same
My Facebook friends, my wonderful Facebook friends.

Unfulfilled Desire

The sonnets I'd write, the poems replete;
and so, I press on, with this unfinished rhyme;
a love unfulfilled, in this moment in time
overdosed on your love my strength, my love
sitting in the dark with the radio the only sound
the honesty of the moment with no one else around.

You just looked away; I doubt you were listening,
you just turned up the radio and you began to sing
the one that you're with I'm going through the
motions, seems that's all I can do when the one that
you're with doesn't realize that it's through.

You got a new style and you're as tickled as a pea
I'm in a mood and I wear it on my sleeve
I work hours over, it's better than being home
I don't seem to care that I left you all alone
damn, I'm tired from feeling this sorrow
forever and ever I am going to miss you girl.

I Keep a Piece of You in Me

I keep a piece of you in me
that no one else will find
I bring it out most everyday
when I need your smile
it's something to think about
when I feel that I need to cry bout
hoping that one day you will reach out
navigating or missing route is
my way of saying I keep you from drought
I really do miss you no doubt
as I keep a piece of you in me.

I Need Your Smile

I need your smile when I need it the most
I need your smile when I feel like I am toast
I need your smile to keep me at hello
I need your smile for the rest of my life
I need your smile kind of like yesterday
I need your smile and that's all I have to say
I need your smile; baby I need your smile.

It Was Like They Opened Up
(A Portal to the Past)

It was like they opened up a portal to the past
but not in the kind of fashion they use to have,
do not listen to your heart, it only tells you lies
as if the treasure comes back to the family in real life,
I hope one day we all can share some light
money doesn't buy us happiness just memories do,
it was like they opened up a portal to the past.

Cut Me Some Slack

Cut me some slack it's just my first day
Cut me some slack I mean no harm
Cut me some slack I only wanted to be your friend
Cut me some slack please, I will do anything
Cut me some slack I am just a little boy
Cut me some slack don't leave me alone
Cut me some slack I am begging you pretty please.

Little Dirty Girl

Little dirty girl your little friend will be happy
Little dirty girl recharge your rear view
Little dirty girl ocean betwixt legs under the bed
Little dirty girl vertical smiles always have a happy ending
Little dirty girl impossible to look away
Little dirty girl marvelous my chat box.

Yesterday's Footprints

Like my memory I miss the
smile from my nightmares
it may take a while to post it
here today, gone tomorrow
from where I was yesterday
times have changed I'm older
than I used to be I've grown
to humor my vocabulary phases
it must be that time of year
where my yesterday's footprints
have been replaced to keep
my innocence and freedom away.

I'll Be There

I will be there for you my friend; I'll always be here
I will be there when you need a friend
I will be there for you to the very end
I will be your friend forever my dear
I will always be here to lend you a hand
I will be there for you my friend; I'll always be here.

A Book on the Shelf

A book on the shelf passed by,
rejected by browsers, ignored
by casual trade, overlooked by readers
often handled but never understood.

A book on the shelf
unwanted and unappreciated
unloved and waits patiently
for that one special among the
others and admire the cover.

A book on the shelf
the quality of the fabric,
its exquisite binding
the handle of the book
feel its weight and worth
if one cares and will
appreciate its quality.

A book on the shelf
when turning the pages,
engage with the contents
understanding its language,

each perfect word on each
pristine page this will be a
story of such worth when it's
found on the shelf.

God is in My...

God is in my fingers
God is in my footsteps
God is in my lips
God is in my voice
God is my protector
God is in my heart
God is my salvation
God is in my life
God is in my world.

Letters in the Library

Letters in the library take my breath away
and filled my world with light. A collection
of letters for each page is part of a remarkable story.
It's the detail on every page of the book that
has my heart full and overflowing with joy.

Love is more than the flashy cover on a book
like an echo in the calligraphy on every page.
letters are returned to sender, but their bounty
was on display with doubts come flooding back
as if the letters in the library have been the same.

So, here I sit in this booth with the letters
in my hand hoping that the letters in a
library can tell me its story.

If I Had to Choose Only One

If I had to choose only one I'd pick that one
If I had to choose only one I know that you are the one
If I had to choose only one I'd give up my turn
If I had to choose only one you would be it.

Dirty Sex

I'm busy doing nothing so get down and
dirty your reload must be fresh and clean
splashed, moans, euphoria, sweat, action.
Wow, that's like a body holiday! Rest
red hot spicy and ready to go. I am a sex
bomb I need you to explode. I'll give you a
great night, I love getting slammed hard
from behind. I'm not going to waste
your time everything will be alright so,
come fuck me and let's have a hell of a night.

If I Had Not Let You Go

If I had not let you go, I wouldn't be in this position
If I had not let you go, I would still have had your love
If I had not let you go, we would be loving parents
If I had not let you go, my world would still be standing
If I had not let you go, you would still be my ride or die girl.

Wet & Charming

Everything you need when the temperature
falls wet & charming
The main thing is wet & charming
Wet & charming tastes are different,
but everybody loves breasts
Sparks fly when it's wet & charming
This is for you when you like it wet & charming
The real fun begins when its wet & charming
Just look at them, they are all wet, wet & charming
One is wet, the second shudders, but both are wet &
    charming
I have a stress prevention ideal when it's wet & charming
when it's wet & charming you need to move to the next
    page.

I Know, I Know

I know, I know, you know it's not too hard
I know, I know, that this is so completely me
I know, I know, that we love ourselves
I know, I know, blah, blah, blah
I know, I know, we all have regrets
I know, I know, I said it once and I'll say it again
I know, I know, you love me, I love you too.

Get ... Out of My Life!!

Get ... out of my life for once and for all
Get ... out of my life forever girl
Get ... out of my life so I can have some peace
Get ... out of my life, leave (get out) right now
Get ... out of my life it's too little too late
Get ... out of my life and be gone for good.

(God Must Have Spent)
A Little More Time On You

God must have spent a little more time on you
as if like life is more than just a dream
God must have spent a little more time on you
as if the friends we keep, the friends we leave
God must have spent a little more time on you
as if we take for granted what we've been given
God must have spent a little more time on you
as if the treasure comes back to you from up above
God must have spent a little more time on you
as if it was like a true never-ending story of love
God must have spent a little more time on you.

I'm Living on Borrowed Time

I'm living on borrowed time
It's not like I want to go
I'm living on borrowed time
well, the rest of your life
I'm living on borrowed time
I'm ready when God calls me home
I'm living on borrowed time
thank you, you guys are my all
I'm living on borrowed time
now I have to go
I'm living on borrowed time
the world must go on without me
I'm living on borrowed time
God take me home
I'm living on borrowed time; yeah,
I'm living on borrowed time.

Stop The Hoax

Stop this damn hoax crap
you rotten son of a bitch.
I am not dead and haven't
died just yet, now you listen
listen up really good because
what I have to say is very
important, you ready? Here it
is now, go fuck yourself over
there and take that damn hoax
site down; have a nice day.

I'll Kick Your Butt
(If You Pinch Me)

I'll kick your butt if you pinch me
this isn't St. Patty's day
I'll kick your butt if you pinch me
even when I am wearing green
I'll kick your butt if you pinch me
when I wasn't even looking
I'll kick your butt if you pinch me
so, don't try to run and impress me
I'll kick your butt if you pinch me.

Every Day Is Precious

Every day is precious, so live it up
Every day is precious, so don't take it for granted
Every day is precious, so be thankful that you're alive
Every day is precious, so thank God that you made it
Every day is precious, when you wake up the next day
Every day is precious, just to see the sunrise
Every day is precious, so make it last.

I Need You Here

I need you here to be with me
I need you here to cuddle me
I need you here to talk to me
I need you here to make love with me
I need you here to be my everything.

A Man Loses Only What He Has

A man loses only what he has
if he is willing to give it up
A man loses only what he has
if he doesn't want it bad enough
A man loses only what he has
even if his odds are stacked against him
A man loses only what he has
even if he is short in low funds
A man loses only what he has.

I'm Not Bipolar (I'm Multipolar)

I'm not bipolar
I'm multipolar
which means I cry and laugh
while I beat the shit
out of you at the
same damn time;
I'm not bipolar
I'm multipolar.

Wise Motherhood

She gave me one from the tree
as I eat the apple from its leaves
a women's work is to clean up afterwards
as she said "I don't need to be fable,
my life to a man's direction" but, to be
hold an order by an opposition of a lover
that I have chosen to marry instead of
to be his servant forever and bow down
to his demands but, if I am his significant other
he will take me as his royal queen she said.

Every Great Discovery, I Ever Made…

Every great discovery, I ever made
I'm blessed with the church of my dreams
Every great discovery, I ever made
I gambled with truth, but asked forgiveness to my sins
Every great discovery, I ever made
I acted on faith, belief, hope, and bravery
Every great discovery, I ever made
just to prove mine and his existence
Every great discovery, I ever made
I'm feeling like I love it each and every day
Every great discovery, I ever made.

You Are Nowhere

You are nowhere
feeling like I love it
ridin' high on cloud nine
yet, somehow still
kickin' it in the backwoods
a secret life with me has
no way of telling so
let's take that drive down
to that dirt road just to
kick up some dust as you're
feeling like you love it
you are, you are nowhere my friend.

Cards I Was Dealt

The cards I was dealt
I'm feeling like I love it
never complain about the
sorry ass cards that were dealt
I just kept on trucking and
give it to the Lord of thee
weather I was battered,
broken, or had a sanctuary to
lay my head down to rest,
I still was forgiven from his
Best, so as the cards are stacked
up against me I'll just play
another hand and let it be.

Signature

Everywhere I go,
everywhere I find,
the signature, the autograph
off of my own handwriting
mixing and mastering
the creative signature move
this is my signature grove.

My Contribution

Written By,
Nicholas Talerico

What Might Have Been

From the road not taken
what might have been
not looking back, for no return
I held a moment in my hand
but in the end, that's what
it should have been or could have been.

I See Pride, I See Power

I see pride, I see power, I see a badass superstar
I see pride, I see power, I see a world from afar
I see pride, I see power, I see the value of a dollar
I see pride, I see power, I see everyone's flaws
I see pride, I see power, I see the greatest writer of all time
I see pride, I see power; I see pride, I see power.

Boom, Boom, Boom,
(It Could've Been You)

Boom, boom, boom, it could've been you,
but I still wouldn't give a shit
Boom, boom, boom, it could've been you,
so, cash me outside how bout dat
Boom, boom, boom, it could've been you,
for the last time who even cares
Boom, boom, boom, it could've been you,
boom shakalaka, so kiss my ass
Boom, boom, boom, it could've been you,
but you still gotta treat it like a credit card
and charge it to the game
Boom, boom, boom, it could've been you,
so, go fuck yourself over there
Boom, boom, boom, it could've been you,
and that's all I have to say about that
Boom, boom, boom, it could've been you.

When Tomorrow Comes

When tomorrow comes, I want to be able to wake up
When tomorrow comes, I want to be next to you
When tomorrow comes, I want to be appreciated
When tomorrow comes, I want to praise your holy
When tomorrow comes, I want to be that man
When tomorrow comes, I want to be that never-ending story
When tomorrow comes, when tomorrow comes.

Can't Go Home

They say home is
where the heart is
but I can't go home
I'm so far gone that
I'm baptized in the
dirty water that is
filled with a bridge
troubled over water

As if I'm like sinking
in quicksand when it's
pulling me under
wishing that I didn't
make that same mistake over
so now, I can't go home
and all I want to do is
go right back home.

I Thought I Told You

Baby girl, I'm hard to love
I thought I told you that
deep inside, I've always felt
that you are my ride or die.

How could I ever hide that
when it was you that I laid
my eyes upon, when in my head
all I could ever see is you?

Dancing when the stars go blue
yes, baby girl, I'm truly in love
with you; I'm really hard to love,
I thought, I thought I told you.

Temporarily Unavailable
(lyrics to My Song)

She said she is
temporarily unavailable
wish I could go back
I never know, I miss it so bad
watching her walk right out
of my life, like it was the first
time when she smiled and said
I'll be temporarily just for a little while.

It's Not Like, I'm Poor

It's not like, I'm poor that I can't help a person in need
It's not like, I'm poor to give back to the community
It's not like, I'm poor to pay it forward to others
It's not like, I'm poor to be snotty or my head up my ass
It's not like, I'm poor to say no and walk away
It's not like, I'm poor, It's not like, I'm poor.

Still Do I Keep My...?

Still do I keep my looks
Still do I keep my dreams
Still do I keep my personalities
Still do I keep my works
Still do I keep my promises
Still do I keep my heart, mind, body, and soul
Still do I keep my dignity
Still do I keep my everything?

The Right Side of History,
The Wrong Side of Learning

I'm on the right side
of history but the
wrong side of learning
but still do I keep my looks,
my identity, my personalities,
or my dreams must work
all against me going viral
with all odds for me and
with this unfinished business
to see, I'm either on the right side
of history or the wrong
side of learning.

Before Winter, I'll Have a New

Before winter, I'll have a new car
Before winter, I'll have a new house
Before winter, I'll have a new poem
Before winter, I'll have a new life
Before winter, I'll have a new world
Before winter, I'll have a new wife
Before winter, I'll have a new change of heart.

I Write What I Think

I write what I think
whether it's originality
or a copywriter to whom
it may concern, it's none
of your business you heard
so, I write what I think
and there's nothin you can
say or make me change that.

I Don't Know How She Does It, But...

I don't know how she does it, but
I sure damn love it though
I don't know how she does it, but
damn she got me buzzin'
I don't know how she does it, but
I'm feeling like I'm lovin it
I don't know how she does it, but
it feels damn good to be hers
I don't know how she does it, but
all I can say is how much I'm appreciated
I don't know how she does it, but
I'm surprised and like wow, lil mamma
I don't know how she does it, but
I'm in love with her heart, mind, body, and soul
I don't know, I don't know how she does it.

Wall Street Goes Global

In other news today
Wall Street goes global
when the world is under
the influences from being broke "O"
Toys "R" Us and Sears have
gone bankrupt uh-oh so now
our political have gotten psycho
as our Wall Street goes global.

I Am Not Your Victim

I am not your victim to play both sides of the field
I am not your victim who is naughty or nice
I am not your victim that has a cold less heart
I am not your victim with those sorry ass cards that were
    dealt
I am not your victim to play the badass role
I am not your victim; I am not your victim.

It'll Be a Thousand Years Before I...

It'll be a thousand years before I cheat
It'll be a thousand years before I lie
It'll be a thousand years before I commit a crime
It'll be a thousand years before I say I'm sorry
It'll be a thousand years before I steal
It'll be a thousand years before I say I do
It'll be a thousand years before I have a kid
It'll be a thousand years before I walk away
It'll be a thousand years before I admit I was wrong
It'll be a thousand years before I say my last regret
It'll be a thousand years before I lay to rest
It'll be a thousand years before I make this my last request.

Tie Me Up, Make Me Scream

Tie me up, make me scream
I got nowhere to run to
just you and me nothin' but
the bedroom and dirty sheets
go ahead girl, jump on this
dick, ride me like a rodeo
nice and slow until I scream
all night long. It's just you and I
until we both start to cream
lean with it rock with it until they
hear us both sing so come on baby
just tie me up and make me scream.

I Need a New Prescription

I need a new prescription
where I can see clearly from love to hate
I need a new prescription
where I can get my head on straight
I need a new prescription
where this world isn't always under construction
I need a new prescription
where I'm not caught between a nightmare or reality
I need a new prescription
where life isn't so politically incorrect
I need a new prescription.

I'll Give You My Love, If You Give Me...

I'll give you my love, if you give me your time
I'll give you my love, if you give me your number
I'll give you my love, if you give me a chance
I'll give you my love, if you give me your heart
I'll give you my love, if you give me your best
I'll give you my love, if you give me your world
I'll give you my love, if you give me your all
I'll give you my love, if you give me everything to hold on to
I'll give you my love, if you give me to be your wife
I'll give you my love, if you give me a happy home
I'll give you my love, if you give me a baby to hold
I'll give you my love, if you give me everything I stand for.

Politically Correct Yes, But I…

Politically correct yes, but I would
rather not say who did it
Politically correct yes, but I would rather keep my opinions
    to myself
Politically correct yes, but I would
rather not kiss and tell
Politically correct yes, but I would
rather keep everything confidential
Politically correct yes, but I am an entertainer, so my words
    don't mean shit
Politically correct yes, but I am sorry that I can't say any more
Politically correct yes, but I am officially no longer yours
Politically correct yes, politically correct no.

Ready or Not

Ready or not
here I come;
tag you're it,
one, two, three,
ready or not
here I come.

You Can Bribe Me With

You can bribe me with your looks
You can bribe me with your tease
You can bribe me with your pretty-please
You can bribe me with your love
You can bribe me with your heart
You can bribe me with your money
You can bribe me with your body
but if you can't be faithful, loyal, or honest
then darling your bribe doesn't cost a thing.

I Am an American, I'm Not a Terrorist

I am an American, I'm not a terrorist
I still don't understand why we have to press one
I am an American, I'm not a terrorist
who believes in all his US Constitutional rights
I am an American, I'm not a terrorist
who proudly waves his flag high
I am an American, I'm not a terrorist
whose opinion should matter when it comes to our incorrect
    political parties
I am an American, I'm not a terrorist
who proudly stands for our freedom as well as our veterans
I am an American, I'm not a terrorist
and that's how I'm going to leave this world
I am an American, I'm not a terrorist.

In The End, I Became

In the end, I became loneliness
In the end, I became broken
In the end, I became numb
In the end, I became shy
In the end, I became fragile
In the end, I became jumpy
In the end, I became scared
But in the end, I became a nobody.

Growing Up Poorly

I was growing up poorly from
place to place even slept outside
in the cold as a kid. I only wanted
a true friend who could understand
my pain, being bullied, picked on,
and thrown to the ground.

As if like most other kids who had
it better with no single parents,
anything their heart desires, only
to dream or wish about like myself
that could ever have wanted in life.

Growing up poorly begging to have
some change just to exchange for a
friendship or two was all I ever knew
as if others couldn't see the true pain
deep within my broken smiles or heart.

And when I cry about something, not
for the attention, but just for some love,
all I got told growing up poorly was if
you cry, I'll give you something to cry
about. So now that I am the black sheep
of the family I sit here alone and write
this poem about how I grew up poorly.

Kinky Boots

Kinky boots is a nickname
that my boss gave me now
that I'm not his hoe anymore.
I am officially his dancing
billboard on the street holding
a sign sayin' senior kinky boots
sign holder guy p.s. I hope to
God that they don't make me say
that I am a sissy, I wear dresses
with a pink thong LMAO SMH
I really hope not LOL kinky boots.

My Shame, Couldn't Let Me

My shame, couldn't let me smile
My shame, couldn't let me down
My shame, couldn't let me fall
My shame, couldn't let me shine bright
My shame, couldn't let me ask why
My shame, couldn't let me find God
My shame, couldn't let me get to my own fame
My shame, couldn't let me be in peace
My shame, couldn't let me breathe
My shame, my shame just likes to destroy my life.

The Reviewers Are Saying

The reviewers are saying it's a number one smash hit
The reviewers are saying it's the best one yet
The reviewers are saying it's off the chain
The reviewers are saying it's a high five-star rating
The reviewers are saying it's a huge seller
The reviewers are saying it's the most epic so far
The reviewers are saying it's everyone's favorite to read about
The reviewers are saying it's New York's best seller of all time
The reviewers are saying, the reviewers are saying it's a yes.

Dear Me, I Hate You

Dear me, I hate you
please go away
p.s. who did you have to
repeat the damn past?

With His Pistol in His Hand

While listening to "Whiskey Lullaby" on the radio
with his pistol in his hand and in the other
hand a picture of his wife, both short
breaded of roses may forever lay down to rest
in his favor God heavily bless on his graceful soul
with his pistol in his hand nobody really
even knows his own true story.

The First Five Pages

I am an old book open and
always there ready to let
you in on all of my secrets
original and full of
imagination, no pictures
just fiction.

Thick with hard covers
a brand new pocket
pretty bookmark stuck
somewhere in the middle
of some rough-sided edges.

I am a notebook college ruled
and very thin trying to fit everything
in I am a pen going as fast as I can
by trying to collect all the thoughts
down on the paper crossing out
ideas and mistakes filled with blue,
red, and black ink that just cannot
be erased.

As I am the first five pages that you
have read with no caption needed
you wrote a poem or two that's
nothing like you, uh-oh I am a fucking
poet who knew as if I was in bed with
a book I am the first five pages you
blew right past.

I'm Thirsty for Your

I'm thirsty for your love
I'm thirsty for your loyalty
I'm thirsty for your honesty
I'm thirsty for your heart
I'm thirsty for your body
I'm thirsty for your soul
I'm thirsty for your everything.

I Didn't Write This

I didn't write this
he did
I didn't write this
she did
I didn't write that
but all in all, I still
didn't write this
hehehe
then who did?

Don't Hit Up My Line

Don't hit up my line if you're drunk
Don't hit up my line if you're horny
Don't hit up my line if you're sorry
Don't hit up my line if you're lonely
Don't hit up my line if you're wasting my time
Don't hit up my line if you're boring
Don't hit up my line if you're crying
Don't hit up my line if you're nothing
Don't hit up my line if you're going to have the sorry ass
    cards that were dealt
So, don't try to hit up my line if you already know
I'm not going to give a fuck.

Today Ain't the Day

Today ain't the day so don't go there
Today ain't the day for your bullshit again
Today ain't the day for any one of y'all's drama fest
Today ain't the day so don't try to test my passions
Today ain't the day to be fucking around
Today ain't the day this is my final warning
Today ain't the day and neither is tomorrow
Today ain't the day so kiss my ass and have a good day
Today ain't the day now go fuck yourself
Today ain't the day, today ain't the day.

She Always Knew

She always knew when I was wrong
She always knew when I was in need of help
She always knew when times get rough
She always knew that I was a fuck up
She always knew that I'd be her ridin' shotgun
She always knew that my words were true
She always knew how much I really love her
She always knew when my love for her was dying to work it
    out
She always knew the song I sang to her
She always knew how much highly I speak of her
She always knew that my world is a true blue wreckage
She always knew, she always knew.

Damn You Lil Hoochie Momma

No class, no respect, no honest
damn you lil hoochie momma
get dressed, get the fuck out, I
can't believe you, this is how
you turned out so grab your shoes,
grab your clothes, grab your purse
and move the fuck out because I
didn't pay for a whore to move in
my house with me so take that fine
ass of yours away from me, man
I hate you fuck dude for real god
damn you lil hoochie momma.

The Private Nightmare with an Ending

The private nightmare
fueled by flame
this storm I became
without recollection or
any self-protection
lacking on poor decision.

It's all fucked up,
a careless excuse
but I know it's not right
for another attempt to
fight the rage inside.

Used to care with or without
help too lost to depend on the
end, a sad reckoning a bad
beckoning when from the start
I should have never had a beginning.

This is my ending, this is my way
too old for begging, talk to you
later this is my final ending, this is
my private nightmare with a sad
and twisting ending.

If You Were My Girl

If you were my girl, I would show you the world
If you were my girl, I would give you my heart
If you were my girl, I would cherish you until the very end
If you were my girl, I would be honored to share your love
If you were my girl, you would be my ride or die girl
If you were my girl, I would never say goodbye my best
    friend
If you were my girl, I'd make her my dream girl
If you were my girl, you would mean everything to me
If you were my girl, you would never go hungry, horny, or
    unhappy
If you were my girl, if you were my girl.

I'll Stop Being a…

I'll stop being an ass
I'll stop being a jerk
I'll stop being a bitch
I'll stop being an idiot
I'll stop being a wastage
I'll stop being a nobody
Nah who the fuck am I kidding?
I am not going to stop being me.

Love Shouldn't Be a Slap in the Face

Can I have a hall pass?
Tell your wife I said hi
love shouldn't be a slap in the face
when you know you should have never lied
now she leads a mixed-up life
oh my, my, my, I wish I can
go back in time because I know I had
fucked up no more second chances with
the ex-wife no wonder why they say
love shouldn't be a slap in the face.

Out of the Blue

Out of the blue you came into my life
Out of the blue you finally apologized
Out of the blue you called me boo
Out of the blue you remembered my name
Out of the blue you shouted I love you
Out of the blue your life came tumbling down
Out of the blue you fell from the sky
Out of the blue you finally kicked the flu
Out of the blue you finally kicked the bucket.

Looking Out, Looking In

Looking out, looking in
I don't see him, nope
I don't seem at all
inside out, outside in
I am traditionally thin
yes, very traditionally slim
inside out, outside in
thank you green eggs and ham
looking in, looking out
I have finally realized what
Dr. Seuss was all about.

I'm On a One-Way Ticket To

I'm on a one-way ticket to hell if I don't get my head straight
I'm on a one-way ticket to go fuck Cody's mom
I'm on a one-way ticket to go fuck yourself
I'm on a one-way ticket to bitch get a job
I'm on a one-way ticket to this is no longer a barstool
I'm on a one-way ticket to getting the fuck about out of here.

Stop Wasting Your Time On

Stop wasting your time on him or her
Stop wasting your time on he said she said
Stop wasting your time on this or that
Stop wasting your time on drama or lies
Stop wasting your time on bullshit or truth
So, stop wasting your own damn time and get a life.

You Are Too Young To

You are too young to drink
You are too young to gamble
You are too young to serve
You are too young to party
You are too young to even know what that means
You are too young; you are way too young.

Girls Are Quick and Dirty When it Comes to...

Girls are quick and dirty when it comes to cheating

Girls are quick and dirty when it comes to lying

Girls are quick and dirty when it comes to playing games

Girls are quick and dirty when it comes to playing both sides

Girls are quick and dirty when it comes to stealing

Girls are quick and dirty when it comes to knowing information

Girls are quick and dirty when it comes to trying to get dirt on someone

Girls are quick and dirty when it comes to being insecure

Girls are quick and dirty when it comes to everything under the sun.

It's Not Very Often

It's not very often that you will see me angry
It's not very often that you will see me cry
It's not very often that you will see me upset
It's not very often that you will see me smile
It's not very often that you will see me hurt
It's not very often that you will see me laugh
It's not very often, it's not very often at all.

Modern Love

You will have your life's mate
written in the book of fate
but you will meet someone that
will become your greatest love.

Although your journeys don't
really connect in your heart
but has a special place that
nobody can ever replace.

And when the time frame is right
he or she will spring right
back into your arms and life
once more again, and your love
will have a happy ending.

Hey Country Girl, This Country Boy

Hey country girl, this country boy
so don't trip just flip your script to
a country boy lil momma and be
my girlfriend more than a redneck
rockstar it's more like my ride or die gal
so hey country girl, this country boy here.

Under Construction

My heart is under construction
trying to build a new bridge after
a handshake that landed a dependable
trust which later got broken and
ran down so now here I am wrapped
around the pole with a caution tap
that says do not enter we are closed due
to being under construction.

It Was Just

It was just a quick call
It was just a short trip
It was just one drink
It was just a picture
It was just an email
It was just a glance
It was just a text
It was just a bite
It was just a joke
It was just a rumor
Just is all it takes to have someone hurt or dead.

Independently I Speak

Independently I speak for myself
Independently I speak for my US Constitutional rights
Independently I speak for my beliefs or religions
Independently I speak for my friends and family
Independently I speak for those around me
Independently I speak up for any given reason to be.

Today I Realized

Today I realized that shit's not free
Today I realized that nobody owes you shit
Today I realized that money doesn't grow on trees
Today I realized that people will hate on your success
Today I realized that hard work pays off
Today I realized that it's just another day.

I Run and I Run

I run and I run until I can't take it any more
I run and I run until life isn't all what it is supposed to be
I run and I run until I cannot help myself any longer
I run and I run until I am tired no more
I run and I run until I've learned my lesson for good
I run and I run until I can't run any more
I run and I run until Jenny tells Forest to stop
I run and I run until the gods give me hope
I run and I run; I run and I run.

Miss Popularity

She's my all-American badass
miss popularity ride or die
southern belle boo thang
who's sexy and she doesn't even
know it, but that's okay
I still love her anyways my miss popularity.

You Must Be Crazy

You must be crazy to fall in love with me
You must be crazy to even I say I love you
You must be crazy to think I am the one for you
You must be crazy to even ask me for intercourse
You must be crazy or hell even weird like me
You must be crazy, damn you must be crazy.

But, I Want to Know

But, I want to know is she available
But, I want to know if it's true
But, I want to know if it's possible
But, I want to know from this moment on
But, I want to know the risk if I take it
But, I want to know all the answers
But, I want to know even if I have to ask
But, I want to know, but, I want to know more.

Is She Available?

Is she available for me?
Is she available to meet?
Is she available to ask on a date?
Is she available at any given time?
Is she available free to go out?
Is she available to be my kind of gal?
Is she available for more than a one-night stand?
Is she available to be my ride or die?
Is she available, is she available?

The Right Side of Hello,
The Wrong Side of Goodbye

You say it first,
then I'll say it back
about that kiss
which led to below the belt
you said I was on the
right side of hello
but, the wrong side of goodbye
yet, again I'm puzzled
by the fact you gave me
a kiss good night and
since then I've never heard
from or seen you ever again.

Typewriter Rodeo

I wrote her letters
using my typewriter,
she wrote me letters
using her heart.

Like a fat kid who
loves cake so high
in the clouds like a
giant in the beanstalk
that made a treehouse
out of wood.

My typewriter skills would
have you off your seats
as if she was riding you
like a rodeo; you feel me?
So, shake that for me as I am
your typewriter rodeo to be.

This Book Has Been Through a Lot

This book has been through a lot
since it's poetry, I imagine it
had trouble finding publishers or
abandoned by book sellers or even
a used dumped owner to profit for
a used bookstore.

My book dream hearted poet looks
fairly readable when I wrote it,
maybe or maybe not though, but I did
find the right spot to read this book
under an oak tree.

As if I like the mild October spring
that fresh country smell with an
open promise to tell, that's why
I said this book must have been
through hell.

Hell Is the Moment

Hell is the moment you realize that you were
ignorant of the fact, when it was true
that you were not yet ruined by desires.

Hell is the moment where the kind of music
I want to continue hearing after I am
dead is the same kind that makes me think
that I will be capable of hearing it then
and forever on.

Hell is the moment.

The Library of Souls

The library of souls
can trip my troll's
it's wicked with a long
winter shivers cold
nobody's story has
have ever been told
but the library of souls
will grip your toes
and drag you beneath
the willow that forever holds.

Blue Dreams

Blue dreams are
like wet dreams
but the difference
between them is
you're not having a
fantasy dream you're
having a fall from a
sky kind of dream
and that my friend
is what you call
a blue dream.

The Deepest Well

The deepest well always had
some type of learning experience
being a dope boy that grew up
with nothin' that's all I ever knew
gotta hustle for a livin' otherwise.

I would have been stuck in the
deepest well with no food or water
and hoping that I make it out
but in the end this is the deepest well
that I had to look down to my scars
just to appreciate life more often.

Walk to Fight for Suicide

I gotta walk to fight for suicide
being bullied and picked on
saying why am I alive?
I am sorry for what all I have
ever done, I do want to make
this right but I am fighting for my life
this is why I have to walk to
fight for suicide otherwise I am
going to die just like the rest
so, walk up to me and make me smile,
make me feel loved, and make me
feel that I want to be part of your world.

Hunger to Save the Epilepsy

I am in need and hungry to
save the ones who have epilepsy,
not only I lost a truly beloved
friend name Mary but I am
trying to save the one who is going to be marrying me.
No, No, why does it have to end this way?
All I want to do is save the epilepsy
from losing another family so please,
please help me to the hunger of
saving the epilepsy.

The New Boyfriend
from My Cheating Girlfriend

new boyfriend: I found your treasure and got your hot girl.

me: Get a fucking grip, you want a cookie?

new boyfriend: Well, kinda. You want the truth?

me: Hell nah, can I have your momma?

new boyfriend: Fuck no.

me: Well then, there is your answer, plus she's yours now.

new boyfriend: I get it. I got the hint but still gonna tell you anyways.

me: [Patting him on the back.] Good luck! [Walking away with a smile.]

new boyfriend: What a dick! [As he mumbled under his breath as I walk away.]

Every Single Thing from My Homie and I

my homie: I need a fucking upgrade on my skills.

me: Da fuck I need a level-up on my game more.

my homie: Yes, I just scored my ticket home.

me: Yeah buddy, you already know it was gonna
be that easy and simple.

my homie: Every single thing is easy, my lil homie.

me: I couldn't even fake it, let's get the fuck out of here.

my homie: Bet.

me: Bet, I am gone.

The Sexy Lingerie

The sexy lingerie is what I adore for each and
every word enraptures the helpless mind
lustful thoughts eclipse, making one blind
completely transfixed, as the reader begins reading
"MORE!" the stroke of the pen, leaves one pleading
rhyme and meter carries you away with desire.
Seductive whispers ignite an unquenchable fire
enticed by words that are both juicy and wet
slowly seduced, the reader begins to sweat
often the culmination is much better than sexual intercourse
as if the poetic lingerie culminating with such intense force.

Oh, No!!!! Not Another Poem

Oh, no!!!! not another poem
It can't be true, he's writing
just to be that brand new
oh well, I guess it's nothing new
so, here is a poem I wrote
just to please you.

Every Man in His Day

Every man in his day has told or retold stories from the past
Every man in his day has at least that one true loyal friend
Every man in his day has held or carried a Bible in hand
Every man in his day has or at least has been cheated on
Every man in his day has cried at least once in his lifetime
Every man in his day has and still carries his wallet
Every man in his day has to face life or death on his own
Every man in his day, every man in his day.

When I Am in Trouble

When I am in trouble I tuck my head down
When I am in trouble I start to stutter
When I am in trouble I lie on someone else
When I am in trouble it wasn't me
When I am in trouble hell I run for the hills
When I am in trouble I am no longer me
When I am in trouble yet this is something you got to see
When I am in trouble I am going to jail
When I am in trouble good night to everyone
When I am in trouble, when I am in trouble.

It's Not as Easy as You

It's not as easy as you think it is
It's not as easy as you imagined it to be
It's not as easy as you hope it would be
It's not as easy as you may know
It's not as easy, It's not as easy as you think.

All She Wants Is That

All she wants is that time
All she wants is that love
All she wants is that energy
All she wants is that loyalty
All she wants is that dick all night long.

Breathing In and Breathing Out

Breathing in and breathing out
taking the time to make a shout-out
doing the hokey pokey and turn
myself around is what it's all about
breathing out and breathing in
this is gotta be the worst since Arron Carter
got kicked out from the Looney Bin
breathing in and breathing out
what else is there to talk about?

Everything But The

Everything but the truth
Everything but the lie
Everything but the honesty
Everything but the loyalty
Everything but the excuses
Everything but the moves
Everything but the stress
Everything but the anything.

A Black Boo

I want an African American
interracial black boo in my life
who can be my ride or die;
no drama, no bullshit mess,
just her and I; only mess we can
have is under those sheets at night.

I want a loyal and faithful type,
she can be thick with them curves too,
mmm my, my, just want a boo thang
to call me her "all mine" all I want is a
black boo; I just want a real black boo.

Butterfly Kisses

The southern belle and her butterfly
are so close, but yet so far away
knowing that each morning she
gets her precious beautiful sunrise
kiss from her one and only ride
or die man, but she is missing her
true butterfly's kiss that wakes up
to her each morning to say rose,
rose, I love you from the bottom
of my heart and I am never gonna
let you go and with his precious
heart he leans over to give her
a wonderful precious butterfly kiss.

I'm Just a Kid From The Projects

I'm just a kid from the projects
coming in hot and heavy gang-
bangers and streetlights was the
only hood style I knew, grew up
poorly I had to hustle like I was
dying, just itching and starching
knowing that I'm starving I'm
just a kid from the projects who
barley knows anybody.

The Book of the Month

Written By,

Nicholas Talerico

The Book of the Month

Attention, attention
fresh off the press,
new book of the month
that you don't want to miss.
Dream Hearted Poet
It's a bad ass pick to read,
get your copy now while
it lasts; it's the latest new hot
thing selling in the streets
so, get your book of the month.

Hot Content

It's great, it's steamy,
it's wet, and it's creamy;
it's a one-time pleasure
so hot that this hot content
has a measure, southern girl
popped off from the charts
as if she was a treasure;
no more heads to be turning
she's mine with a hot content
of a brand-new meaning
my vocabulary is burning
omg, omg, she is my hot
content naughty.

She's My Baby Girl

She's my baby girl from the first
day that I held you in my arms
I knew nothing else really even
Mattered.

You're wrapped around daddy's
little finger as if you know that
his heart is forever yours.

You may have your daddy's looks
but you get your brains from
your mother, baby girl, don't
you ever forget it either.

Yes, baby girl it's just you and I
against the world and when I'm
dead and gone just remember that
you are the queen.

And I will forever live on; yes,
you are always my little girl
as I tell everyone including the
world that she's my baby girl.

I Make My Husband

I make my husband watch and then clean me up afterwards
I make my husband cook, clean, and bathe for me
I make my husband obey, be a house maid, and stay-home
    dad
I make my husband feel, taste, touch, hear, and smell
I make my husband do anything that I want him to do.

Welcome to My Life

Welcome to my life where
my childhood experience
has taught me and shaped
me to the person I am today.

I've become a stronger and
wiser person and still until
this day my life will never be
the same, so welcome to the
hell of my life.

I Love Being Honest

I love being honest cause that's who I am
I love being honest cause I am too faithful
I love being honest even if it hurts someone's feelings
I love being honest just to get my pleasure from it
I love being honest even ask my mother
I love being honest and that's never going to change.

Good Looking Out, Good Looking In

Good looking out,
but that's not what it's about.
Good looking in,
let's find you a spot.
Good looking out, good looking in;
and turn yourself all about.
Good looking out,
so we can hop on pop
just to change his route.
Good looking in,
as we are hand in hand
with fingers and thumbs
just to match his amount.
Good looking in, good looking out,
finally, she is peacefully out.

Oh, The Places You'll Go!

Oh, the places you'll go
will make you a winner of all time.
Oh, the places you'll go
to get fame yes, you'll be famous as famous can be.
Oh, the places you'll go
will just let you grow, grow up to be a bigger seed.
Oh, the places you'll go
it will be great any direction you go.
Oh, the places you'll go
except when you don't, because sometimes you won't.
Oh, the places you'll go
everyone and you will be waiting for a yes or no.
Oh, the places you'll go,
oh, the places you'll go.

Temporarily Blocked

I am temporarily blocked from Facebook
I am temporarily blocked from Messenger
I am temporarily blocked from talking to her
I am temporarily blocked from the world
I am temporarily blocked from everything and anything
I am temporarily blocked and I am temporarily unavailable.

Somebody Scream

Somebody scream
Somebody shout
Somebody shake it all about
Somebody scream and cry for help.

Living With The Devil

Living with the devil that has no fear
Living with the devil who tries to take over
Living with the devil that has tricks and turns
Living with the devil will take your soul
Living with the devil that's all I ever know
Living with the devil, living with the devil.

If I Get Locked Up

If I get locked up make sure that I don't have anything on me
If I get locked up give my daughter a sincere apology
If I get locked up can I trust you to be there in the end
If I get locked up please don't be unfaithful to me
If I get locked up take me away with the handcuffs
If I get locked up will you still be there for me?

Digital Storytelling

In pictures and in words
this digital storytelling is
quite the most spontaneously
epic reading of all time
so, go buy your copy today
and let's all work in a bind.

From Street Life to Country Life

From street life to country life
your playground is my jail time;
memories from the past have me
kicking my own dumb ass
from ghetto to white trash I still
can back that ass up when some
one acts like an ass, so from
street life to country life your
playground is my jail time.

Wherever You Are
(My Love Will Find You)

Wherever you are my love
will find you as if I wanted
you more than you ever
know, so I sent love to follow
you wherever you go
forever and ever I will always
be proud of you no matter
wherever you go I will
always have you.

I Feel Like a Retired Rockstar

I feel like a retired rockstar
with the same old story to tell
as if I am on a train going
nowhere bound for some kind
of hell; I am all washed up
with nothin' new to even try to sell.
I feel like a retired rockstar who
wants to scream and yell.

Full, Full, Full of Love

In another life, I'd make you mine
or find a way to be full, full, full of love.

Like a waterfall floating down a stream of its
amazing scenery with full, full, full of love.

With Dad and Mom's kiss, hug, and love nothing
is greater than or full of full, full, full of love.

And with a sheet of paper and pen I can feel
the urge to write again with full, full, full of love.

You're Tired, You're Poor

Your house is on fire
your children are gone
you're tired, you're poor
but you say you got nothin' left
yet you ran from the past
as if you were lost like an
American drifter who was lost
at sea ,now you see the light
hoping that it will give you hope
to a brighter night
you're tired, you're poor and so am I.

Fuck Me

I was under the bridge with
my empty pockets told the day
smiles from the geese floating
on by the streets are crossed
and over to the dead end

My phone is nothing but a piece of shit
fuck you I need a fuck me drink
somebody pass the dictionary please
my head is ready to find the killing floor
beyond my depths is calling out a siren
choir fuck me, fuck me again once more.

Yours

You're cloaked in red
I recognize your game,
you're in need for perversion
of the written word
your silence is a blessing
with only a pen and red ink,
your words go unspoken
with things you'll never understand
in this silent world of yours.
I repeat, I repeat, I am yours.

Awful Poetry From What I Have Read

When I first started doing poetry, I was awful
I still am awful, but I'm less awful than my poetry
reflects my life, awful—sort of I didn't read all
of the Bible I think I read a few books, namely
the ones I could actually read, it's not always true,
is what I'm typing but then again, sometimes it really
is just a piss-poor luck excuse I had.

Having to settle for what they got, but normal
people make their life, like a writer makes a
poem, I said I knew this girl that wanted to tell
me her life story and still remember the man;
he was in another lifetime reminiscing all
the years I've spent as she said the thoughts I had
will forever be bad as my poetry still sucks like trash.

Orchestrating Love

Words silently speak
between hearts and minds
as if it was playing strings
and spades at the same time
orchestrating love was the
game we called life.

There is no room for
disagreement there is no
room for you to challenge
what I tell you cause you're
all mine as if I am demonstrating
the orchestra love in real life;
I am, we are, husband and wife
orchestrating love, now good night.

On This Battlefield Called Life

On this battlefield called life
I struggle day by day just
to survive, my PTSD kicks in
as if I have some kind of suicidal
thoughts; social media I had to
experiment just to show everyone
that bullying still doesn't stop;
still here I am getting picked on
please stop, so I can move on
but that's still not going to stop
this is why I hold onto everything I got
as I live for this battlefield called life.

She's Just Too Hot

She's out of your league
she's not your type
she's every man's dream
yet she's just too hot
to even call mine.

My Booty Is

My booty is skinny
My booty is round
My booty is flat
My booty is curved
My booty is all the above
My booty has all the girl's wanting to moan.

When It's Over You'll Be

When it's over you'll be looking back
When it's over you'll be saying, "Damn, I made it!"
When it's over you'll be happy you did it
When it's over you'll be amazed on how well you achieved
When it's over you'll be successful.

My Current Occupation

My current occupation is my God
My current occupation is my wife
My current occupation is my child
My current occupation is my mother
My current occupation is my job
My current occupation is my home
All my current occupations are run by life.

Here Fishy, Fishy, Fish

Here fishy, fishy, fish
I got some nice food for you.
Here fishy, fishy, fish
I promise I won't eat you.
Here fishy, fishy, fish
come to papa.
Here fishy, fishy, fish
yes, I finally got you.
Here fishy, fishy, fish.

Just remember, fish are friends not food.

Yep—Fake, Fake, Fake

Yep, yep you are
fake, fake, fake
nope, nope, I will not
take, take, take
cause to me you are nothin'
but fake, fake, fake.

An Honest Homeless Person

An honest homeless person
walked up to me the other day
and asked me if I can spare
some change; he just needed a
dollar to drink his pain away.

I kindly declined his offer
as he said sorry and thanks
anyways and with such kind
words he made I walked up
to him and said here is some change;
he gave me a hug and said thanks.

And God bless as if there was nothing
more that I can give; I smiled and
took him in later on in life. God has
blessed him as he payed it forward
to another honest homeless person.

Your Orgasm Inside Me

I want your orgasm inside of me
right now, nice and creamy
fill me, fill me pretty please
I want you to release it all in me
so deep that it's nice and steamy
I want, I want your orgasm inside of me.

I Married You, Not Your Family

I married you, not your family
if I wanted their opinion I would
have already told you, so leave me
the fuck alone and take that drama
elsewhere pretty please.

This Southern Boy Is Thinking About

This southern boy is thinking about church
This southern boy is thinking about God
This southern boy is thinking about a nice cold beer
This southern boy is thinking about his truck
This southern boy is thinking about his southern belle
This southern boy is thinking about his rebel flag
This southern boy is thinking about his family
This southern boy is thinking about his life
This southern boy is thinking about everything under the
    sun.

Country Girl Lawd Have Mercy

Inside peanut butter, outside Hershey
body like a back road
country girl lookin' like
lawd have mercy
I gotta camouflage cutie
that's packing a little booty
how you gonna rate that
when she's still ridin' shotgun
head over heels as she's
my country girl lawd have mercy.

From Society Page to the Front Page

From society page to the front page
this huge spotlight hasn't really changed
I am who I am so go check my resume
it's not always about the pay it's all about
my fan base so from society page to the
front page I am forever the same.

I'd Like to Fill Her Up
(But My Thing's Too Small)

Yesterday my best friend slash home girl
sent me a serious text message saying
her ex old boyfriend sent a text message
to her new man saying that I'd like to
fill her up but my thing's too small, lol he replied.

As If I shook my head and text her
back saying I have just lost it and I don't
know why, but this is the funniest shit I've
heard all day as if we both agreed that
he's never going to change so I told her
to delete his number as she said okay.

It's Like Livin' in A

It's like livin' in a trailer park
it's like livin' in a one-bedroom studio
it's like livin' in a huge mansion
it's like livin' in a gold world like God.

Redneck Country Girl

I got this redneck country girl who
reminds me of Little Red Riding Hood
so damn sweet but still miss understood
yes, I am her Big Bad Wolf that likes
to whistle at her and try to blow her
house down but instead she kidnapped me
as if I was her ride or die backwoods
southern belle beauty queen.

It Is to Be

It is to be broken
It is to be torn open
It is to be healing
It is to be reached
It is to be in my mouth like salt
It is to be with such delight
It is to be everything you dreamed of
It is to be the power of thanks
It is to be a discipline for knowledge.

Do Not Be Ashamed

To escape that you are guilty
you must have misread the complex
instructions, you are not a
member you lost your card or you
never really even had one.

Their eyes are on your letters and books
their hands are in your pockets
their ears are wired to your bed
so, don't be so quick to be ashamed.

Reading the page you have made,
your history will leave you ashamed
but I am not ashamed I have said,
however, I have this gut feeling that
there is some sort of a vertical geography
portioned in my life as if a man has
put his history to sleep I once have said
so, do not be ashamed I once read.

She's

She takes her clothes off
She lies naked upon the bed
She places her hands over her part
She gives us all equal kisses
She moans loud upon her making
She betrays art with life
She makes her heart open to the public
as she makes another life reappear.

I Wanna Be Your Cowboy

I wanna be your cowboy
I wanna be your knight
I wanna be your man
I wanna be your husband
I wanna be your everything
as long as I wanna be your cowboy.

The Storyteller

For years, I lived on a diet of your words,
letters, diaries, the collected works, until
they dropped from my mouth like alcohol
for each time I spoke my friends could
smell it on my breath

I took the journeys you took, I've
walked with you on those tracks
which lead me to being your wife
I have spoken in your dreams,
I have eaten your heart with those tricks

You slipped through my facts as we slept
in the same house under my bed sheets
as if I helped you restore your pictures that
brought your books back just to discover
the missing key to your precious desk

As if the storyteller all the sudden says
I am not what you think, this is not
what I wanted and in the end I'm
felt with my heartaches; I was foolish
to marry the woman in my dreams which
now leads to heaven, I am in heaven he said.

The Young Prostitute

My only books, are your mother's looks
just as beautiful like some women
the seductive kind as a dark eyed whore
passionate, cruel honey-lipped, syphilitic
wild side that is with a once in a lifetime
rare gift, but if you're not careful
she will spit in my face, turn her back
like a cold face mistress on a broken stem,
which later those come pretty cheap in time.

The Dream Catcher

Bring me all of your dreams,
you dreamers,
bring me all of your dreams
so I can keep and catch
the falling sleepless dreamers
as if I dream all of my dreams
as I am the dream catcher to all
of your wonderful dreams.

Love Is Like Whiskey

Love is like whiskey
love is like sweet red wine
you got to love it all the time.

Love is like whiskey
love is like sweet red wine
it's just never going to die.

Love is like whiskey
love is like sweet red wine
cheers, bottoms up, this is how we live life.

Love is like whiskey
love is like sweet red wine
I miss you my dear wife.

Love is like whiskey
love is like sweet red wine
and now it's time to say goodbye.

Love is like whiskey
love is like sweet red wine.

Baby 'O' Baby

Baby 'o' baby
help me please
I'm down and out
baby 'o' baby
I'm a po' guy
that nobody cares about.

Everybody Loves My Baby

Everybody loves my baby
but my baby doesn't love
nobody but me.

Everybody wants my baby
but my baby doesn't want
nobody but me and only me.

Putting In The Seed

You came to fetch me
as if I expected you like a visitor
that sweet soft kiss which
led the wanting of you inside my bed
under the fire and the silver moonlight
beneath my hand I can feel you
creeping up of the crafting my heart
against your chest bumping and grinding
until I squeeze a little ink drops in your nest
putting in the seed as I am hoping
to make it last while we watch it grow
until we both turn into ash
God bless, God bless in the name of his flesh.

Sidewalk Celebrity

I am Mr. Hollywood
I am Mr. Rich but not to blame
poetry, poetry walk a fame
sidewalk celebrity is the name
TMZ and newscast members
asking me questions for the day
I hope, I hope you remember
this country boy who said he's
got so much creativity yes indeed,
I am your sidewalk celebrity.

The Thought of Someone Else

The thought of someone else in your arms really scares me

The thought of someone else calling you baby has me falling hard

The thought of someone else having our baby makes me feel unsecure

The thought of someone else marrying you has me wanting to cry

The thought of someone else saying she's my ride or die boo has me dying deep inside.

To Be Liked by You, Would Be

To be liked by you, would be cool if you sure did
To be liked by you, would be a hell of an honor
To be liked by you, I would be most amazed and surprised
To be liked by you, I would be such a popular guy
To be liked by you, I would be the happiest person alive.

Baby
(Gimmie A Little Lovin')

Baby gimmie a little lovin'
and put that sugar on my tongue
Baby gimmie a little lovin'
on a train that runs somewhere
Baby gimmie a little lovin'
make sure it's short and a sweet loving
Baby gimmie a little lovin'
inside peanut butter, outside Hershey
Baby gimmie a little lovin'
so, I squeeze a little ink drops in your nest
Baby gimmie a little lovin'
and gimmie, gimmie some sugar.

I Reckon It'll Be

I reckon it'll be the last time with you
I reckon it'll be your last time being late
I reckon it'll be the last time you lay in my bed
I reckon it'll be the last time that you ever lie to me
I reckon it'll be the only time I ever beat on you.

I Was Thirsty, She Was Hot

I was thirsty,
she was hot,
I kissed my girl
with a soft tender kiss;
my thirst was quenched
I can breathe again
oh my god, damn she fine;
can we do that again
one more time?
I was thirsty, she was hot.

My Heart Is Not

My heart is not a mirror;
you cannot peer in it.

My heart is not a toy;
you cannot hide the pain.

My heart is not a stone;
you cannot turn it over.

My heart is not a mat;
you cannot roll it up.

Haven't Slept With A Woman

Haven't slept with a woman
who hasn't given birth to my newborn child.
Haven't slept with a woman
who hasn't even said yes to marrying my dumbass.
Haven't slept with a woman
who hasn't even asked me on a date yet.
Haven't slept with a woman
who hasn't even met my goofy ridiculous clown ass.

(Do Not) Sell Me Out Baby

Do not sell me out baby,
please do not sell me out;
do not sell me out baby,
do not sell me out.
I used to believe in you baby
now I begin to doubt.

Still I can't help lovin' you
even though you did me wrong.
Still I can't help lovin' you,
I can't help lovin' you,
though you did me wrong
even though you did me wrong.

I want to tell you bout that woman
my used-to-be, she was really mean
she was really, really mean
my used-to-be, my used-to-be
I want to tell you bout that woman
who used-to-be, my used-to-be
so, baby, do not sell me out pretty please, please.

This I Write, Mix Ink with Tears

This I write, mix ink with tears
written for grief before I become grievously
to tell the pain, to tell the fears
to even tell you my own sorrowful tears
unfinished story with no excuses
how sharp pain you caused me for all these years
now here is my final thought for what
you have done it is what it is and
now finally, I moved on as if
this I write, mix ink with tears.

The Unfaithful Wife

I took her to the river
believing she was single
but coming to find out
that she had a husband.

Making love in a garden nude…
ah summer long your lover's
arms and ass are bare in the air
as if like the devil who is a
trickster without a cause.

With her peaches and my cream
slipping, sliding, blowing, and gliding
ultimately forgetting that the woman
who I slept with later to find out
I impregnated or procreated with.

Reading between the lines
of the unfaithful wife later to
find out that her husband died.

The Greyhound Affair

I met this mad talking shit
beautiful woman from
Greyhound station; it started
off as a glance, later on
getting head while traveling
to our destination sitting
next to me hoping that I got
the chance, later on that day
I got in her pants, she bought
me pizza and asked me to dance;
we got back on the bus and
went our separate ways, nine months
later oh shit she's having
my kid, the end.

Just A Kid from Kankakee

I'm just a kid from Kankakee
who's from the projects that
grew up poorly hustling like
I'm starving so I gotta eat
from the streets to the country
I'm just a kid who's from Kankakee.

As I Ride, As I Ride
(Down That Road Called Life)

I picked up my life and took it with
I picked up my life and took it on a train
as I ride, as I ride down that road called life
like passengers on yesterday's train
tired of looking out the same window on today's world
in other words I guess, it's never the same
when life can be so harsh and cruel
as I ride, as I ride down that road called life.

Written While Drunk

This was written while drunk
I really don't give a fuck
so, cause you really suck
now run along or you're going
to get dunked
this was written, this was written
while being drunk.

Riddle from the Book

Riddle me this,
riddle me that,
I come to climb
on your jungle hat

Riddle me this,
riddle me that,
I am not going
to ask you that

Riddle me this,
riddle me that,
please can you
tell my buddy Matt

Riddle me this,
riddle me that,
I just want to know
if you are really fat

Riddle me this,
riddle me that,
this is a book that
will make you laugh

Riddle me this,
riddle me that,
now it's time to
say my goodbye
riddle me this, riddle me that.

When I Got You, I Thought

When I got you, I thought everything would be ok
When I got you, I thought we would last forever
When I got you, I thought you would be my ride or die
When I got you, I thought my world would never end
When I got you, I thought I would forever have you.

My Life Ain't Nothin'
(From a Nightmare of a Dream)

My life ain't nothin'
from a nightmare of a dream
I never had no kids
I never had no wife
to even take my life
I'm just a poor boy doomed
deeper than a whistle
louder than a cry
worse than a scream
and even more horrible than not being heard
my life ain't nothin'
from a nightmare of a dream.

Little Black Boys in a Southern Jail

Little black boys in a southern jail
singing the country blues just to
make some kind of noise that most
people never really heard of as if
it was like little black boys, little
black boys who even knew that song.

Home Is Where the Heart Is

Where my home is, my bed is,
where my woman is, and my kids are
for all the dreams we've dreamed
for all the hopes we've held
for all the songs we've sung
for all the flags we've hung
home is still where the heart belongs.

I Want You to Have His Baby

I just wanna
make your water
BREAK!!
I just wanna
feel your water
BREAK!!
let me POKE THE BABY!
I want you to have his baby
please give me that baby.

Sex Is on Your Mind

You can't control your hormones
sex is on your mind,
you've been feeling kinda lonely
since your man left you behind,
oh lawd, I done forgot what it's like
to have sexual intercourse all the time,
give it to me, give it to me
one last ride so, take my hand and
ride me like a rodeo until
you can't control your hormones no more
because sex is on your mind.

She's My 5150

She's my 5150 anything
she says goes
smokin' hot baby look at me go
I'm stylin' and so
she's got me on a tightrope
that doesn't mean that
I would say fuck
the main boo when nobody
knows you it's hard to
make friends where you gotta
fit in anywhere you can
go with the flow, be part of the plan
we're a small pack so take a chance
as she's my 5150 ride or die main boo.

Stay Away from My Chick

Stay away from my chick
she doesn't want your dick
if you don't I'm gonna shoot you, in the head,
cause I can't wait to see you dead
you drive me nuts, you make me sick
so, stay the fuck away from my chick.

Makin' You Mine

I'm makin' you mine
as if I hit it full throttle
to the bottle in reverse
for the words I meant to say.

I'm stuck in a hole that's
hard to control digging
myself deeper with lose
of courage to tell you that
I want to make you mine.

My vocabulary has never
been miss spoken before
hoping that I can score
cause all I want is you.

I keep trying to change
your mind as I keep
wanting to make you mine.

Don't Eat With Your Dirty Hands

Don't eat with your dirty hands and
expect me to give you a clean plate;
washing your hands is the proper way
so, take a seat, be patient, and say a prayer,
but for the love of God please don't
eat with your dirty hands in my kitchen.

I Got Carried Away in the Moment

I got carried away in the moment
not thinking about my surroundings
I got carried away in the moment
not seeing who's in front or behind of me
I got carried away in the moment
and not even given any fucks about myself
I got carried away in the moment.

Southern on Display

Southern on display
as if life was a game
sort of like a model
for every risk I had to take
there's always a mistake
just to be a southern on display.

Supercalifragilisticexpialidocious

supercalifragilisticexpialidocious is
a long descriptive poetry word known
to many, none of which can pronounce
or spell it correctly.

The Dirty Thought

The dirty thought that
runs through my head
has people asking me
if I should get help
as I tell them no I am
good just having one of
those dirty thoughts again.

When I Grow Up, I'm Going to Be Like

When I grow up, I'm going to be like you
When I grow up, I'm going to be like him
When I grow up, I'm going to be like God
When I grow up, I'm going to be like my hero
When I grow up, I'm going to be like everyone under the
    sun.

(God Must Have Spent)
A Little More Time On You

Written By,
Nicholas Talerico

The Original Nudist

You are lovely, you are my soul
you were so beloved, you were so sweethearted
you were so recalled, you were true loneliness
you were the original nudist.

She'll Make Your

She'll make your day
She'll make your heartbeat jump
She'll make your kid
She'll make your food
She'll make your sex drive go insane
She'll make your world
She'll make your life a living hell.

While Tracking Mud Into The House

While tracking mud into the house
I can see my wife's facial expression
on her face hoping that she will
forgive this puppy-dog face with many
words to say besides that I love you
give me a sweet gentle soft southern kiss
and be on your way as I said yes baby
while tracking mud into the house.

But, Tomorrow I Will Redeem My...

But, tomorrow I will redeem my memory
But, tomorrow I will redeem my tickets
But, tomorrow I will redeem my prize
But, tomorrow I will redeem my rewards
But, tomorrow I will redeem my past history
But, tomorrow I will redeem my everything.

The Book Performers

The book performers are raw like
a glass marble bank; the record
never changes when it's always
the same every single flippin' year.

Slim odds on sneaking back into
the children's book even though
they record all of the old fragments
from rookie of the year to even today.

Either way the book performers
are raw like a glass marble bank.

I'm Spontaneously in Love

I'm spontaneously in love with you
I'm spontaneously in love with your eyes
I'm spontaneously in love with your body
I'm spontaneously in love with your personality
I'm spontaneously in love with your sex drive
I'm spontaneously in love with the way you do.

If Only She Could

If only she could see through my flaws
If only she could tell how much I need her
If only she could feel how lonely I am
If only she could touch my lips once more again
If only she could hear how much I miss her
If only she could taste my breakfast in bed again
Either way, she's gone and now I have to move on.

I'm Just an Asshole

I'm just an asshole that everyone is going to hate
I'm just an asshole that everybody is going to love
I'm just an asshole that nobody appreciates
I'm just an asshole and I am never going to change
I'm just an asshole, I'm just an asshole.

I Have This Letter You Wrote Me

It's been ten years now and I still
have this letter you wrote to me.
It seems that God has spent a little
more time on you than me.

Looking back now, I'm glad it
ended this way even though I
wouldn't change a damn thing.
It was your personality that
got to me, not your looks, honey.

Your smile that weakened my knees,
your passion for horses that got
me thinking, you're perfect in every
man's dream, yet here I am today
describing my broken heart scene.

From the birthday card to the
gangster hat, even the long-
lasting memories I had; either
way, you still got me to smile
and I want to thank you for that,
so here I am ten years later
reading this letter you wrote me.

She's That Kind of Gal Who Kept

She's that kind of gal who kept
her head in the clouds
She's that kind of gal who kept
her secrets hiding in a box
She's that kind of gal who kept
her ears open and her mouth shut
She's that kind of gal who kept
her dreams safe from the world
She's that kind of gal who kept
a country boy from telling
She's that kind of gal who kept
a Bible under her pillow at night
She's that kind of gal who kept
her word every time she prayed to the Lord
She's that kind of gal who kept
everything to her own self
She's that kind of gal who got the best
of me with her precious smile.

Must Have Been Yesterday

I started feeling this a way
I've been waitin' and a wantin'
it must have been yesterday
ain't worth even a little bit
I know it ain't today
must have been yesterday
it should have been today.

I'll Find A Chance To

I'll find a chance to say I am sorry
I'll find a chance to say I love you
I'll find a chance to say I want to fuck you
I'll find a chance to say let's get married
I'll find a chance to say I want to grow old with you.

I Still Appreciate You

I still appreciate you when the time we had was real
I still appreciate you even though you did me wrong
I still appreciate you because that's how I was raised
I still appreciate you no matter which way it ended
I still appreciate you, I'll forever appreciate you.

I Used to Tell You

I used to tell you my secrets
I used to tell you my fantasies
I used to tell you my dreams
I used to tell you anything under the sheets.

I No Longer See You As

I no longer see you as my ride or die
I no longer see you as my girlfriend or wife
I no longer see you as the person I can trust
I no longer see you as the one I slept in bed with
I no longer see you as anything but a friend.

Your Answer Is

Your answer is yes
Your answer is no
Your answer is maybe
Your answer is sometimes
Your answer is I don't care
Your answer is so
Your answer is who cares
So, if your answer is all of this
then why should I even bother?

I'm Standing On

I'm standing on a burning bridge
I'm standing on the edge of glory
I'm standing on the back of the seat
I'm standing on someone else's grave
I'm standing on my own two feet.

Backwoods Booty

Southern momma with
a backwoods booty
so big I thought she's
a cutie everyone thought
I was literally crazy
5150 country girl twerking
on me ok, I have to
admit it she's every man's
dream southern born
southern bred this is not
a dream; I repeat this is
not a dream, damn, I can't
wait to see her shake
that backwoods booty for me.

You Know What Time It Is When...

you get called by your full name after dark.
supper time is ready.
you got in trouble for dumb shit.
you look at your watch waiting for the bell to ring.
everyone else is ready to go except you.

Pretty, Pretty, Little Liar

pretty, pretty, little liar
I bet that pants are on fire
pretty, pretty, little liar
no need for you to be even hired
pretty, pretty, little liar
that's ok I know you're wired
pretty, pretty, little liar
you must have to retire
pretty, pretty, little liar
this is my way of saying you're a liar.

Don't Just Listen

Don't just listen
take some action
be part of someone's
total reaction.

People Say I'm Black

White people say I'm black
black people say I'm white
mexican people say I'm mixed
and other people say I fit in;
in other words, we all bleed the same
that's why some people don't stay
in their own lane people say
people say I'm black and that's
never going to change.

Seriously, Between Us

Seriously, between us
go ahead I won't tell.
Seriously, between us
I don't hear anything, I don't see anything.
Seriously, between us.

My Flag, My Roots, My Camo In My Boots

My flag, my roots, my camo in my boots
I'm a southern Illinois country boy asshole
who's from the woods and smokes a little weed
you mess with me, I can guarantee you will
not succeed while I'm kickin' ass and takin'
names just to proceed my flag, my roots,
my camo in my boots is all I'm ever going to need.

Excuse Me, Pardon Me Miss

Excuse me, pardon me miss
you're drinking my cold beer
this country girl doesn't care
she loves some southern hick-
hop rappers two sticks and a
apple will keep the doctor away
she said to me so I grab two
to enter and three to unlock this
country girl's wildest beast it could
be all yours she said as I say
excuse me, pardon me miss,
but you're still holding my beer.

One Tree Hill

Tree hill is the place
where I want to be, so
beautiful and nice to see,
some people were nice
and some people were
mean. Wilmington, NC,
has got the best beach
parties, excuse me miss
pardon me, I'm just
here for the weekend
to meet and greet my tree
hill family as if this
is the place I want to be;
my one tree hill family.

I'll Just Keep Writing

I'll just write until my right hand falls off
I'll just keep writing with mind or no mind
I'll just keep writing as if I had a predetermined doubt
I'll write as if I had a cause
I'll write past the time that I should have quit
I'll just keep writing smack dab down the middle
I'll keep, keep writing nonstop all day long
I'll just keep writing, while y'all keep on hating.

My Craigslist Dream

My Craigslist dream
was to find someone
who can swing, a little
buck, a little wild, somewhere
in between that can drink,
hell, even can show me a
thing or two snap, pop,
and crack holy shit she
knew how to Bing damn,
now she's my Craigslist dream.

Broken Crayons

We're a box of colored crayons
a little bent... a little broken
from life's uses and abuses
from cruel words some may have
spoken were so disappointed
because we've never known success
every would have been dream has ended,
every hope has left no address
you see, I, too, was once as broken
yes, I was, also, once as blue,
but I still color that picture with
a broken crayon.

Bam! It's A Good Thing! (That! I Did It)

Bam! it's a good thing! that! I did it
it's like, bam, we've been getting it
bam reserved from the winning
it's like, bam, it's a good thing! that! I did it
it's bam! and bam! and bam! and bam
and bam is a good thing! that we did it.

Hip-Hop Isn't Dead

Hip-hop isn't dead
it's something that you do;
rap are just the words
that are inside of you.

You are my poetry,
poetry is my life;
tell me, how will I survive
now that I can no longer write?

In your eyes I see my redemption;
it's a pinpoint of light that
has an exception cut so deeply
that I was blinded by my own ambition.

Forbidden chances filled with
doubt and unsatisfied visions
lost with a creative imagination
that forever having people say
that hip-hop still isn't dead.

I Still Believe in Christmas

I still believe in Christmas
I still believe in love
I still believe the message sent to us from above
I still believe in miracles; each new day opens one
I still believe in Christmas
Yeah, I still believe in Christmas.

Cotton Candy Christmas

You're like cotton candy Christmas
so sweet yet I still see the childish
games you play; this has got to stop
so my sins were blacker than yours
have ever been what that got to
do with the price of butter of jewels?

The person that I was back then has a
brand-new identity now; listen here
and listen up well you cotton candy
Christmas get yourself in check before
I go off the walls on you my dear, now
have a wonderful cotton candy Christmas
and God bless.

Rumor Has It

The rumor has it that you have a girlfriend
The rumor has it that you just had a baby
The rumor has it that you're getting married
The rumor has it that you're a cheater
The rumor has it that you're a liar
The rumor has it that you're going nowhere
The rumor has it, the rumor has it.

She'll Always Be

She'll always be that young beautiful lady
She'll always be my best friend
She'll always be my lover
She'll always be my soulmate
She'll always be that wonderful wife
She'll always be the mother of my child
She'll always be my growing old pain in the ass
She'll always be my ride or die
And she'll always be mine forever.

It's Not Like Her

It's not like her to steal from me
It's not like her to lie to me
It's not like her to cheat on me
It's not like her to even call me
It's not like her to say I am sorry
It's not like her to admit saying I love you
It's not like her and it really never has been her.

Changing Me

If I can take it all back I would
but to be honest, my past has
changed me. Feeling emotional
is something I can only look forward
to hearing myself sob in the middle
of the night has gotten me closer to God.

Praying that I hope he takes me
for all the wrongs that I've been
doing begging for a second chance
to forgive me the abuse, the rape,
the physical, and the emotional
violence that was done to me.

I know karma is a bitch that has
caught up to me. God I can't describe
enough how I'm sorry feeling the
pain with guilt and the torture but I
guess this is the way life has to be.

And I know people say I'm nothing
more than just a dreamer but that's
okay because that is the part
where it's changing me.

Motivation Speech

Almost seven a.m. and I'm ready to start
this change in my life. If you're not
here to help me grow I don't need
you around. It's 2017 it's all about
my dreams; I know haters are going
to hate gotta treat it like a credit card
charge it to the game while everyone
else is fighting the alligators and
I'm over here cleaning the swamp.
Don't forget to tell the boss man
I got another job so help all those
who are poor and in need, you never
know their struggle until you bleed.

Love is Love

All you need to do is grab an Apple Crisp
twist flip shake and bump it make sure
those seeds and worms are out of it cause
you don't want to eat the bad from it, well
then that's the way I think about it when love
is love then, so take a lesson from me and
learn from it.

Not all love is bad when you get to know
Someone, so grab their hand and tell them you
love them and some cause at the end of the day
you'll never know if it's gonna be the last of
them. Love is love and God bless everyone.

It Was Only A Kiss

It was only a kiss
that just got lost in a moment
It was only a kiss
that didn't mean anything
It was only a kiss
I was a little bent and a little broken
It was only a kiss
don't you really understand?
It was only a kiss; it was only a kiss.

Low Self-Esteem

I hear a thousand words about me
and it makes no difference
but yet, I hear an insult
and all my confidence goes to shit.

Black Girls Rock

Black girls rock
black girls rock
all them black girls
know how to make
their man say damn
black girls rock
black girls rock
I love it when all the
black girls rock.

Holy Thursday

The bloody Bible and
the bloodiest gospel
gives me a true reason
to believe it's a holy Thursday;
God's word, God's sacrifice
should always be on a
holy Thursday.

So and So Is Lying

So and so is lying about me
So and so is lying just to have revenge
So and so is lying there's no butts to it
So and so is lying and it's never going to stop
So and so is lying; so and so is always lying.

It's Always the Wife

It's always the wife who cooks and cleans
It's always the wife who caters to her husband
It's always the wife who is a stay-home mother
It's always the wife who cares for her children
It's always the wife who bitches and moans
It's always the wife who believes in God
It's always the wife who prays at night
It's always the wife's job to do all those things at one time.

Be Like Me

Be like me;
stay true, stay humbled,
stay blessed, and stay original.
Nobody wants a copycat
who can't be like me;
be like me.

You're Not Talking

You're not talking to me anymore
and I still don't know why
it seems like you went ghost on
me for a little while.

I keep a pen and a pad of paper
to jot down all the reasons
why, but here I am still puzzled
asking God to forgive me.

So, I can ask you why now that
I know you're not talking
to me anymore, at least I got
to know the real reason why,
so, here is a kiss for
my goodbye and I am
out of your way.

Love Unknown

Your heart was foul
your heart was hard
your heart was dull
even though my lips went cold

My heart fell behind
yes, indeed I was lacking from
the state of mind

As I fell faster for the
love of unknown I am hoping
that I get a shot at your love
that is well known

So, love me known
love me tender
just don't leave me with
your love unknown.

I Found A Girl to Be in Love

I found a girl to be in love
with her lips that are red-hot
like glowing charcoal in the
midday rising sun

I found a girl to be in love
with her hips so damn curvy
like a backroad almost going
a 45

I found a girl to be in love
with her personality that
sparked like a firework
on a Fourth of July summer

I found a girl to be in love
with her kinky and wild side
no man on earth can resist her
body that's a beauty charmer

I found a girl to be in love
I found a girl to be in love with.

Jenny Kissed Me

Jenny kissed me
as if I was in the
movie *Forest Gump;*
so sexy that I wanted
to run away;
country boy, country girl,
how stupid can we
be? Jenny reached over
and decided to kiss me.

Bonnie & Clyde

She's cheaper to keep her
kinda like Bonnie & Clyde;
always and forever to be
my ride "N" die pull up a rocker
and stay for a little while;
I can show you this lifestyle
that you never had lil mamma
so, stick with me as we
ride or die together just like
back in the day when Bonnie
& Clyde took over the world.

Verse Idea

I'm just a kid from Kankakee
everybody wants to know me
sidewalk celebrity yes, indeed
country boy who's putting in the seed
I feel like a retired rockstar
who's living the dream.

She Tosses That (Boom, Boom)

She tosses that boom, boom
so far in the air that got you saying
you've got to be kidding me
I want her to circle jerk on me
that boom, boom has to taste so sweet
damn, baby girl come shake it for me
while she tosses that boom, boom
now everyone wants a piece.

Liar, Liar, Pants On Fire

Liar, liar, pants on fire
I told her she looks hot
liar, liar, pants on fire
I told her she's got a candy-ass
liar, liar, pants on fire
I even told her she can be my man
liar, liar, pants on fire
hell, she can even have my kid
liar, liar, pants on fire
now our relationship is over
liar, liar, pants on fire
and I guess I got to find a new girl
liar, liar, pants on fire.

Reflections From An Abused Kid

From broken promises to broken homes
my reflections from an abused kid
have twenty-six years of domestic violence that
have me looking in the rearview mirror
and wondering where I've been

It's just another thing to me as if most
others would have committed suicide;
it's really not a joke to those who are
fighting for their life just to stay alive

What helped me just to stay alive was
my poems, my music, and some good
friends that helped me escape from
my negative thoughts who knew that
this is coming from a person who has
reflections from an abused kid.

My Life # 5

1999
My ninth year of my life
I was at a ballpark when I decided
to feed and chase the ducks. Well what
happened was I went to bend over and
the duck came up, bit me on my ass,
and started to chase me as I was screaming.

2000
My tenth year of my life
was a pretty brutal year for me. One,
I didn't see where I was going and ran into
the damn stop sign; two, I forgot that the
library doors weren't sliding doors and I ran
right into it. And last but not least, I went
to the doc because there was a tick on my dick.

2001
My eleventh year of my life
wasn't really cool. The story of it came true:
my brother and sister decided to put it on
and as they came back and once I turned
my back, they were dressed up as a clown with
a knife in hand. I screamed and freaked out that I
literally ran and slept under my mom's bed for a week.

No Such Thing As A Bad Kid

There is no such thing as a bad kid,
you just have to have a one-on-one
talk and make sure they learn from
right to wrong; as I say there is no
such thing as a bad kid.

My Life # 6

2002
My twelfth year of my life
was starting to get more rough. I was being
tossed and flipped on a glass table from
not only my mom but my father as well.

2003
My thirteenth year of my life
I was sent to an independent living group
home for bad behavior boys and girls
because I had gone off and tripped my trolley.

2004
My fourteenth year of my life
I came home from a visit where I decided to
hang out with a buddy and get high and drunk.
Well, we thought it was cool to chase each
other outside and in the end, my dumbass
tripped over a rock and landed in our laundry
room window, which later landed me to the ER.

Gossip Friendship Talk

Bestie: So, what's the story on you and your ex-husband?

Girlfriend: There is no story.

Bestie: So, why is he still in town?

Girlfriend: I don't know why he's in town, I'm not speaking to him.

Bestie: Was there other women on his troubled list?

Girlfriend: I don't know, I don't care. Let's go do something!

Bestie: Ok, I am down. Let's go.

Her Face, Her Tongue, Her Ass

Her face, her tongue, her ass
have me hypnotized; the walk
she does has me saying damn
oh my, my, let her sit on my face
and I can make her mine, mine, mine.

The Girl He Likes

The girl he likes is a polished hoe
The girl he likes is a mud cricket
The girl he likes is an unlikely match
The girl he likes is a hunchback whore
The girl he likes is my fucked-up ex.

I Didn't Want It To Be A Craigslist Moment

I didn't want it to be a Craigslist moment
but I had to post it
I didn't want it to be a Craigslist moment
but you had me feeling this way
I didn't want it to be a Craigslist moment
but I felt that it was needed
I didn't want it to be a Craigslist moment
but I was hoping you have read it
I didn't want it to be a Craigslist moment
but you have found it
I didn't want it to be a Craigslist moment
but I was thinking you were the same kind of different as me
Now that it was a Craigslist moment, you got to me now.

You've Got To Be

You've got to be fucking kidding me
You've got to be serious
You've got to be kidding, right
You've got to be shitting me
You've got to be, you've got to be joking.

I'm Not Bigfoot Where You Can...

run up to me and act like you're Kongo.
put a net around me and to try trap me.
think I am afraid of you.
say damn he's big, I want to ride him.
trick me into having a beef jerky.
try to go out and find my missing ass.

Uncle Sam Wants You To....

Uncle Sam wants you to pay your taxes
Uncle Sam wants you to join the army
Uncle Sam wants you to be part of his crew
Uncle Sam wants you to take everything you own
Uncle Sam wants you to vote for your president.

A Clownlike Fool

Clownlike hands
on a common
sense with two
thumbs down and
no mode to tell

Wrapping yourself
like a fool
hoping to create a
ripple between
me and you

As you say I am
vertical to me
as I say well-done
mate you finally got
a clean slate

And with your face
now I can move on
to the next final place.

O My Great Idiot

O my great idiot
O brother where art thou?
Holy Thursday
and you said you were out
but when I looked
you were in stocked, I shocked
my head and said
O brother O my great idiot
how dumb can you get?

Between This Wish and That Wish

Between this wish and that wish
it still doesn't add up to what I want.
Between this wish and that wish
I wonder which one I will choose first.
Between this wish and that wish
does it really even matter, it's all the same.
Between this wish and that wish
and everyone else's wish makes it hard for me.

From Time to Time

From time to time
I want to cry
From time to time
I want to laugh
From time to time
I want to cringe
From time to time
I want to be loved
From time to time
I want to be alone
From time to time
I want to do it all over again.

I Had This Wet Dream

I had this wet dream
about these two black beautiful queens,
both very thickums and a
light colored cream
who even thought that they both
be laying naked in my bed
sucking and fucking both of my heads
as I try not to moan and scream
oh, shit I woke up and had to pee
thanks a lot now I hate this day
because I really had this wet dream.

While You Were Out

While you were out I did the household chores
While you were out I did all of the cooking
While you were out I babysat your kids
While you were out I became friends of family
While you were out I gave you some extra cash
While you were out I made a private phone call.

Dirt On My Boots

I got dirt on my boots
from all the mud, sweat,
and tears that I do on
a daily, so what if I get paid
doing the same shit regularly
because in the end it's not
going to be buried with me
that's why I'm proud to get
a little dirt on my boots.

If You Ask Me

If you ask me I might say yes
If you ask me I might say no
If you ask me I might say maybe
If you ask me I might tell you
If you ask me then you will know.

I'm Ok, You're My Parents

I'm ok, you're my parents
coming from an abused kid
who's holding back all the
tears from his eyes.

Tread marks sharply written
all up and down his arms as
he's deeply in bars studying
hard as if he's ready to fight
his own battle scars.

It's okay, God is calling me
home, so he takes his sharp
pointed comb and a string of
rope and takes his own life.

The next thing we knew he
was gone as his parents say I'm okay.

Just When I Thought...

Just when I thought it couldn't get any worse
Just when I thought it was about over
Just when I thought it couldn't get any better
Just when I thought it was my time
Just when I thought; just when I thought.

I Was Too Young To Notice

I was too young to notice that they were having sex
I was too young to notice that they were drinking
I was too young to notice what were drugs
I was too young to notice the meaning of gambling
I was too young to notice any of those things.

Under My Bed

Under my bed there's a monster
Under my bed there's the floor
Under my bed there's a couple of toys
Under my bed there's a Bible
Under my bed there's nothing but a story to tell.

Sometimes In The Summer There's

Sometimes in the summer there's
an October fall
Sometimes in the summer there's
an overnight thunderstorm
Sometimes in the summer there's
an extremely hot day
Sometimes in the summer there's
nothing to do at all.

When She Walks Right By Me

When she walks right by me I can taste her lips
When she walks right by me I fall right out of my chair
When she walks right by me I can see her smile
When she walks right by me I know I got the hots for her
When she walks right by me I can tell she's the one
When she walks right by me I know I got a legit backwoods
    booty.

This Time, I Thought

This time, I thought it was over
This time, I thought it would be the last time
This time, I thought I could catch a break
This time, I thought everything would be fine
This time, I thought this would be the last book I wrote
This time, I thought oh wait I was lying
This time, I thought; this time, I thought.